Working with Trans Survivors of Sexual Violence

of related interest

Written on the Body
Letters from Trans and Non-Binary Survivors of
Sexual Assault and Domestic Violence
Edited by Lexie Bean
Foreword and additional pieces by Dean Spade, Nyala Moon,
Alex Valdes, Sawyer DeVuyst, and Ieshai Bailey
ISBN 978 1 78592 746 1
eISBN 978 1 78450 517 2

How to Understand Your Gender
A Practical Guide for Exploring Who You Are
Alex Iantaffi and Meg-John Barker
Foreword by S. Bear Bergman
ISBN 978 1 78592 746 1
eISBN 978 1 78450 517 2

Trans Voices
Becoming Who You Are
Declan Henry
Foreword by Professor Stephen Whittle, OBE
Afterword by Jane Fae
ISBN 978 1 78592 240 4
eISBN 978 1 78450 520 2

Working with Trans Survivors of Sexual Violence

A Guide for Professionals

Sally Rymer
& Valentina Cartei

Jessica Kingsley *Publishers*
London and Philadelphia

First published in 2019
by Jessica Kingsley Publishers
73 Collier Street
London N1 9BE, UK
and
400 Market Street, Suite 400
Philadelphia, PA 19106, USA

www.jkp.com

Library of Congress Cataloging in Publication Data
A CIP catalog record for this book is available from the Library of Congress

British Library Cataloguing in Publication Data
A CIP catalogue record for this book is available from the British Library

ISBN 978 1 78592 760 7
eISBN 978 1 78450 618 6

Printed and bound in the United States

Contents

Introduction

Research on trans people's experiences of sexual violence[1] has grown considerably in the past decade. Although limited in number, studies show that trans[2] people may confront similar, if not higher, levels of sexual violence and abuse (James *et al.* 2016; McNeil *et al.* 2012; Grant *et al.* 2011).

---

1 'Sexual violence' is an all-encompassing term that refers to any sexual act or activity which is unwanted. This includes sexual contact and behaviours that take place without consent or understanding. As explained by Rape Crisis England & Wales (RCEW), 'There are many different kinds of sexual violence, including but not restricted to: rape, sexual assault, child sexual abuse, sexual harassment, rape within marriage/relationships, forced marriage, so-called honour-based violence, female genital mutilation, trafficking, sexual exploitation, and ritual abuse. Sexual violence can be perpetrated by a complete stranger, or by someone known and even trusted, such as a friend, colleague, family member, partner or ex-partner. Sexual violence can happen to anyone. No-one ever deserves or asks for it to happen. One hundred per cent of the responsibility for any act of sexual violence lies with its perpetrator. There is no excuse for sexual violence; it can never be justified, it can never be explained away and there is no context in which it is valid, understandable or acceptable' (RCEW website 2018).

2 In this book we use the term 'trans' or 'transgender' to refer to anyone who does not identify with the gender they were assigned at birth. This may include those who have transitioned from one binary gender (male/female) to the other, and those who identify outside these binary genders. See Chapter 1 and the Glossary of Terms at the end of the book for more details on the gender-related terms used in this book.

The devastating effects of sexual violence on individuals, including trans individuals, can be mitigated by effective responses from health and well-being professionals and organisations. Professionals are also in a frontline position to act and prevent abuse. However, professional courses in the health and sexual violence support sectors do not usually provide specific training about working with trans individuals or communities. In addition, due to the interpersonal betrayal and complex effects associated with sexual violence and abuse, as well as previous experience of discrimination experienced in response to their gender identity and expression, many trans people are unlikely to raise the topic on their own. These factors often leave professionals lacking skills and experience in talking about sexual violence with trans individuals and working with them to help them heal.

This book focuses on building the capacity of professionals and organisations as means of bolstering systems of accountability for sexual violence and facilitating recovery for trans survivors. Many of you will work in mainstream services which serve primarily cisgender[3] people, but may occasionally find yourself working with trans clients. Some of you who will find the book useful will work in specialist organisations that focus on trans people, some of whom may have experienced sexual violence.

Our interest in the needs and experiences of transgender survivors arose when we were both involved with Survivors Network, the Rape Crisis Centre for Sussex, which is based in Brighton & Hove, a city well known for its large lesbian, gay, bisexual and transgender plus (LGBT+) population. The trans community has a visible and vibrant presence locally. Following a trans awareness

---

3   'Cisgender' refers to anyone who is not transgender. See Chapter 1 for more details.

training session for staff and volunteers of the Rape Crisis Centre, we wanted to understand more about how our centre could better meet the needs of the trans survivors in our local area. We found that very little research on this topic existed, so in 2015 we conducted research with trans survivors and the professionals working with them, to explore specific barriers for trans individuals in accessing support within the United Kingdom (UK) after an experience of sexual violence (Rymer and Cartei 2015).

Through this research, we learned first-hand some of the challenges that trans survivors were facing as they struggled to access mainstream and specialist services. Our conversation turned to how we could draw on trans survivors' experiences, and on our own experience of working with survivors, to improve the response of service providers and professionals so that trans survivors' needs were heard and responded to. As part of this work, we have been involved in establishing a national helpline for trans survivors of sexual violence, which will be discussed in more detail in Chapter 7.

It is against this backdrop that the idea for this book came to be. In fact, many of the themes and suggestions for best practice developed in this book stem directly from the stories shared by those who took part in our study, as well as those who we had the privilege to work with in the years that followed. You will find in this book many quotes from trans survivors who contributed to our original study. You will also find anonymous quotes from trans survivors who contributed to a survey specifically for this book. Their contributions can be found in the 'Trans voices' boxes throughout this book. We would also like to recognise the valuable contributions of other organisations, researchers and activists on this topic. Rape Crisis Scotland, for example, has taken a keen interest in supporting trans survivors and has developed guidance for other Rape Crisis Centres on the inclusion of trans women in women's services (Rape Crisis Scotland 2011). Forge, a charity in the United States (US), has conducted valuable research into the experiences of trans survivors and has produced useful guidance documents for professionals who work with them (munson and Cook-Daniels 2015, 2016).

Weaving together survivors' accounts with professional knowledge and best practice, this book aims to provide clear explanations, practical suggestions and support for professionals and organisations that want to make their services more inclusive for trans individuals who have experienced any form of sexual violence or abuse, no matter how or when it happened.

Chapter 1: An Introduction to Trans Identities will be helpful for professionals who would like to start or increase cultural competency in trans issues. It offers an introduction into different trans identities as well as the transition process, and the differences between sex, sexuality and gender. It also gives you tools you can use immediately such as do's and don'ts for behaviour and language.

In order to specifically address our interest and rationale for this book, *Chapter 2: Violence Experienced by the Trans Community* outlines the multiple forms of disadvantage and oppression faced by many trans people, including increased vulnerability to sexual violence. This chapter will provide insight into the intersectional discrimination and violence faced by the trans community. Understanding the level and impact of these experiences of violence, both on the individual and on the whole trans community, is essential in understanding the barriers that trans survivors face when accessing services and how organisations and professionals can best support trans survivors.

Chapter 3: Trauma and Its Effects describes common experiences survivors may encounter immediately following or long after a sexually traumatic experience. The chapter first considers what it means when human suffering becomes trauma, and ends with an overview of common responses, with reference to neurobiological processes explained in accessible language. It also looks at individual and societal factors that may influence the impact of, and recovery from, trauma, emphasising that individuals experience sexual trauma in different ways, and one path to recovery and healing that is right for one person may not necessarily be right for another.

While trans people appear to be at a particularly high risk of sexual violence, they may also find it more difficult to access services that would be able and willing to support them in their recovery. *Chapter 4: Problems with Accessing Mainstream Services* looks at why it is often difficult for trans people to access services from specialist organisations and generic providers in the aftermath of sexual violence and how those services can become more inclusive of trans clients.

The two chapters that follow include recommendations for all levels of service delivery, from organisational policies (*Chapter 5: Best Practice: Organisations*) to advice for frontline professionals (*Chapter 6: Best Practice: Individual Practitioners*) so that your communication can be positive, non-stigmatising and successful. These chapters also contain practical tools, such as an accessibility audit, and key advice for different professionals.

In the final chapter, *Chapter 7: Looking Ahead*, we conclude with a reflection on the role of service providers, with particular focus on the LGBT community and specialist sexual violence organisations to create a landscape where trans survivors are no longer constrained by narrow perceptions and expectations of gender when accessing services, and where diverse gender expressions are visible and valued. This chapter includes a discussion about the need for better access to services for non-binary survivors specifically, who often find themselves unable to access support in the current service provision landscape, which mostly serves binary gendered people.

Some chapters may offer suggestions or recommendations that appear in more than one chapter or reference another chapter. In these cases, the topics are distinct enough, in our opinion, to warrant separate chapters, despite the fact that some of the same recommendations could apply to all. In other cases, recommendations are omitted from chapters if they are already noted in some other chapters; readers are directed throughout the book on appropriate chapters to cross-reference and review. This book is designed ideally to be read in full, cover-to-cover, but it is also possible to dip into chapters that seem particularly relevant to your specific work.

It is our hope that this book will become an important tool for a variety of professionals who work with trans survivors of sexual violence, including, but not exclusively, rape crisis workers, counsellors/therapists, independent sexual violence advocates, police officers, solicitors, doctors and nurses, social workers, and health and well-being practitioners. It should be read in conjunction with guidance documents developed by professional bodies for mental health and sexual violence support professionals that complement this guide (see the Further Reading section at the end of this book).

By equipping you as a professional we hope to help improve services for a community that not only suffers violence at a disproportionate rate but also often does not receive safe and supportive services deal with the aftermath of this violence.

Chapter 1
An Introduction to Trans Identities

Introduction

This chapter aims to offer you basic background information about what it means to be transgender. It will give you an idea of the huge variety of gender identities among people who identify with the term 'transgender' or 'trans'. The chapter will also provide information about the processes of transitioning from a gender you are assigned at birth to one with which you identify more fully. At the end of the book, you will find the Glossary of Terms, which you may wish to refer to as you learn about trans identities and as you read the rest of this book.

Development of gender identity

For many people and across most cultures, gender forms an important part of how we understand ourselves and how we group people into social categories. Your gender has a massive influence on what others expect of you – of how you act, your roles in relationships, how you dress, the way in which you walk or speak; the list is nearly endless. Your gender also impacts how you understand your own identity and experiences across your lifetime.

These expectations are set very early in one's life, often before a child is even born. Medical professionals offer to tell expectant parents their child's sex early in pregnancy with the assumption that this information will convey some essential and important information about who their child will be. In reality, the only information being shared is about one aspect of the sex of a foetus. One's sex 'refers to various qualities displayed by the human body that, strictly medically speaking, define people as being male, female, or intersex' (TransWhat? 2017). These qualities include many different physical characteristics, including genitalia, hormone levels, chromosomes, internal sex organs and secondary sex characteristics. When a medical professional tells expectant parents that they are 'having a boy', they are basing that assumption on one aspect of the foetus's sex (their genitalia). Quite often, a link is then made between this very basic information and a range of other complex assumptions we link with it.

This is when the term 'gender' comes into play. Gender is not synonymous with sex. The World Health Organization defines gender as:

> the socially constructed characteristics of women and men – such as norms, roles and relationships of and between groups of women and men. It varies from society to society and can be changed. While most people are born either male or female, they are taught appropriate norms and behaviours – including how they should interact with others of the same or opposite sex within households, communities and work places. When individuals or groups do not 'fit' established gender norms they often face stigma, discriminatory practices or social exclusion. (World Health Organization 2017)

While some gender-related expectations are biologically based, such as the exclusive ability of those with female sex organs to give birth to another human being, most gender-related expectations are culturally constructed and change over time. For example, in Western culture no longer than a century ago it was unacceptable for women to wear trousers but this is now an everyday and unremarkable occurrence. However, a man wearing a dress is still a significant deviation from culturally imposed gender expectations.

Continuing with our example, depending on their own social and cultural experiences, their values, and their own gender-related experiences, these parents could have a whole range of expectations of their child after being told by medical professionals that he is a boy. These parents will inevitably communicate many of these expectations to their child in both overt and subtle ways. If their child defies these expectations, the parents may react with concern, confusion or even anger.

The child himself will learn from a very young age that he is a boy and that this means he needs to do certain things in certain ways – and that he is not to do other things. He will learn this largely by observation of his parents, his peers, other adults and the media. Occasionally, he may be given clear verbal instruction about how he should behave given his gender: 'Boys don't cry', 'Ladies go first', 'Boys don't wear makeup', and so on. Meanwhile, he will be developing his own sense of who he is and how he wants to express himself in relation to his gender. This is his *gender identity*. He may never think about this explicitly but it is likely to emerge for him at times when the gender-related expectations of others are at odds with what feels true, natural or right for him. These may be more subtle deviations from 'the norm' (for example, 'Why can't I play with the dolls just because I am a boy?') or very significant ones ('I feel deep discomfort when I am called a boy').

For many people, these moments of friction between their own gender identity and society's gendered expectations lead to them finding ways of stretching and adapting the gender they were assigned at birth so that it feels right to them. Over time, Western society has become more tolerant to this stretching, and the boundaries around how women and men 'should' look and behave have widened substantially. Individuals who continue to identify with the sex and gender they were assigned at birth despite these moments of friction are known as *cisgender*.

For other individuals, this friction is not something that arises only in specific incidents, but a reality that permeates their day-to-day life. They may feel this friction in social circumstances when the gender-related expectations of them are at odds with their authentic self. They may also feel this friction when relating to their own body, particularly the primary or secondary sex characteristics of their body.

For these individuals, the friction they feel is so strong, so uncomfortable and so unbearable that it is likely to cause the individual deep distress. This distress is often called *gender dysphoria*. For them, there is a deep sense of disconnect between their own gender identity and the gender or sex they were assigned at birth. These individuals may identify as *transgender*.

Diversity of gender identities

The way in which sexes and genders are categorised and described is culturally dictated. In most modern Western societies, sex and gender are usually understood to exist in two 'binary opposites' –

male and female. These categories are also often assumed to be absolutes and that any individual can only be designated to one or the other. Other cultures have a wider range of sex and gender descriptors, although most also include these two 'binary genders'. For example, in Navajo culture, in addition to male and female gender identities, a 'third gender' exists. This gender is often referred to as 'two-spirited' and individuals of this gender are considered to encompass both male and female in one person (Public Broadcasting Service 2015).

Some transgender individuals transition from one 'binary gender' to the other. A person who was assigned female at birth and then transitions to live as a man is a transgender man or a *trans man*. Similarly, a person who was assigned male at birth and transitions to live as a woman is a transgender woman or a *trans woman*.

For other individuals, the binary system of gender does not provide an adequate way to describe their own gender identity. They identify somewhere between or beyond this binary system. Two broad terms currently in common use for individuals who identify this way are *non-binary* and *genderqueer*. The glossary at the end of this book contains a list of terms for a variety of other gender identities which lie between or beyond the binary genders of male and female. Regardless of the terms any of us use to describe our own gender identities, what remains true for all people is that our gender identity is an intensely personal and self-defined part of our identity.

Coming out

Many individuals who are not cisgender will at some point decide to 'come out' to others about their gender identity. Because we live in a society where everyone is expected to identify comfortably with the gender they were assigned at birth, it is often necessary for transgender (including non-binary) individuals to come out so that their internal experiences and understanding of their gender identity can be understood by others.

Trans individuals who come out in adolescence or adulthood are likely to have spent a great deal of time coming to understand their own gender identity. It is no small thing to tell other people that you are transgender. For most people, doing so takes immense courage and conviction. Coming out risks exposing oneself to violence, harassment and hurtful or insensitive reactions or questions. But it can bring freedom too and a chance to be honest to who you actually are, and ideally it will also create opportunities to be truly seen and understood by others.

Trans voices: experiences of coming out

'When I told my mother, she was initially very supportive. But when I changed my name, she told me she would rather call me "nothing at all"! She is no longer in my life and my sister has only just come back into it after a year and a half of silence and absence. But my kids have been wonderful, and my friends have mostly been very accepting.'

'My family disowned me. I haven't spoken to them in four years. I never came out to my community but I am lucky I live in a nice area so it's not bad at all. Luckily, I moved in here when I had been transitioned for four years. My ex couldn't cope with my lower surgery so ended things three days after getting home from stage 1 lower surgery (initial surgery to change one's genitalia).'

'Everyone was completely accepting, with the exception of one individual. My brothers immediately started referring to me as their sister and my mother called me her daughter. Old habits of using masculine pronouns took a bit longer to overcome, but there was never any malicious intent. Only once such incident caused embarrassment, and that was when a friend introduced me to a new neighbour as "he".'

'I reached out first to a therapist when I was a teenager; she avoided the topic almost to discourage that kind of thinking. It took me a while to build up that courage, so it was heartbreaking. I eventually managed to come out to university friends and was met very warmly. I came out to my family later and when they supported me I was fine with everyone knowing. Coming out has drastically improved my life in all kinds of unexpected ways.'

Some transgender individuals recognise and come out about their transgender identity as children. This can be from a very young age, although there is no 'typical' pathway for a transgender child. For these children, their coming out experience will be impacted in an important and lasting way by the way in which their parents react to the child's gender identity. Some parents are able to understand and embrace their child's gender identity and support the child in expressing this identity in a way which feels honest to and positive for the child. Other parents strongly reject their child's transgender identity and will go to great lengths to force their child into a more mainstream expression of their gender. This may cause their child a lot of suffering and force them to suppress their feelings of gender dysphoria, which may re-emerge later in life. Many parents exist somewhere in the middle of this spectrum. Moreover, parents' own understanding of and reaction to their child's gender will be greatly influenced by the culture and community in which they live.

Transitioning

After coming out, many transgender people will choose to undergo some sort of transition so that they are more able to express their gender identity in day-to-day life. In popular culture, 'transition' is generally understood to entail 'sex realignment surgery', a category of medical procedure which enables transgender people to alter their bodies so that they align better with one of the binary sexes. For some people, this is part of their transition, but there is no requirement for trans individuals to undergo surgery of any kind. Indeed, there are a whole host of other ways in which transgender individuals transition.

Social transition

Most transgender individuals undergo a lengthy and ongoing social transition for some time. This part of their transition focuses on expressing their gender identity in a social context and having their gender identity recognised by others. One aspect of this part of transition is coming out to important people in their life – family, friends, colleagues and so on. Transgender individuals may also want to or find they need to come out to a variety of institutions, such as schools, colleges or universities, GP surgeries, banks, insurance companies and central government.

Many transgender individuals change their name as part of their transition and they will need to inform people of this and ask that they start using their chosen name. They may need to remind people continuously of this or even face people who refuse to use their chosen name. Similarly, some transgender people change the pronouns they use to refer to themselves. Trans men (those assigned female at birth but who identify as men) may transition from using 'she/her' to 'he/him'. Trans women (those assigned male at birth who identify as women) may move from using 'he/him' to 'she/her'. Many genderqueer or non-binary people choose to use the gender-neutral 'they/them' pronouns. Some people choose to use other gender-neutral pronouns such as 'ze/zer' or 'xe/xyr'. The pronoun 'it' should never be used to describe a trans or non-binary person (or any person for that matter!) unless the person has made it clear that 'it' is their own chosen pronoun.

Transgender people also often change the way they present themselves physically by changing things such as how they dress, any makeup they might use and how they cut or style their hair. They may use special compression vests in order to achieve a flatter chest (a practice called binding) or they may begin wearing prosthetic breasts. They may also learn ways of walking, standing, sitting, and so on that better match their gender identity.

Within their social transition, transgender individuals may start to utilise public services or spaces that align with their gender identity. For example, they may start to use toilets or locker rooms that match their gender identity. If they are living in single-sex accommodation, they may move into accommodation that matches their gender identity.

Physical and medical transition

As previously stated, many transgender people (but by no means all) choose to undergo some form of physical or medical transition. Such transitions are typically done in order to alter either genital anatomy and appearance or to change secondary sex characteristics (for example, breasts, hair growth, voice pitch). These changes are generally achieved through surgery, hormone treatment or interventions such as voice coaching.

Before receiving medical treatment for their physical transition, transgender individuals generally have to undergo extensive assessment by psychiatrists or psychologists. The purpose of this is to ensure individuals are 'really sure' about making such lasting and impactful changes to their bodies. While some people find this process helpful, many find it quite distressing and oppressive to be asked to 'prove' their gender identity and evidence the need for what to many is life-saving and life-altering treatment. This assessment is typically done within gender identity clinics, run by the NHS, but it can be done privately as well. The process can also take years, which results in delays in treatment. This can prolong and even worsen the gender dysphoria experienced by trans people. While the majority of gender reassignment treatment is available on the NHS, the long waiting lists for many procedures lead to some individuals paying for private treatment, either within the UK or internationally. Those who cannot afford the cost of private treatment and who also cannot afford psychologically to endure such long waiting times may choose to access treatment outside the medical system, for example by purchasing hormones online.

Hormone treatments are widely used by transgender people. Hormones can have dramatic effects on secondary sex characteristics. They generally lead to changes in body fat distribution, voice pitch, hair growth, and skin softness and thickness. Female hormones can lead to increased breast tissue, and male hormones can lead to a decrease in breast size. Hormones can also have an impact on one's sex drive, energy levels and mood.

Pre-pubescent transgender children may utilise hormone blockers. These pause puberty so that transgender children do not have to undergo such an extensive medical transition as adults and in order to avoid the dysphoria and distress that puberty can cause transgender children. This treatment is heavily regulated, and children who wish to use hormone blockers are subject to thorough assessment before they are prescribed. If a child comes off hormone blockers, puberty progresses, so it is a reversible treatment.

There is a large range of surgical procedures on offer to transgender individuals. What, if any, surgery an individual chooses to have is a very personal decision. Contrary to what is often portrayed in popular culture, there is no single surgery or combination of surgeries which 'makes' someone a man or a woman.

Some surgical procedures focus on secondary sex characteristics. For example, transgender people may have breast reductions/ mastectomies or breast implants. This is often referred to as '*top surgery*'. Facial surgery is a possibility in order to achieve things like softening of the jaw line, enlarging one's lips or changes to one's nose. It is also possible to have genital surgery (often called '*bottom surgery*') in order to change one's genitals. There are a variety of options for such surgery and, again, what options are chosen is a very individual decision.

Trans voices: medical transition

'I started testosterone earlier this year and have been referred for top surgery. Both of these things have made me feel more comfortable in myself and allowed me to be seen as my gender identity rather than my assigned gender.'

'It was absolutely critical to my well-being. I had experienced intense gender dysphoria since early childhood relating to both primary and secondary sex characteristics.

Physical transition had a negative impact on my sexual relationship (with my heterosexual wife) but we've found ways to adapt and are still very much together.'

'I haven't physically transitioned in any way, but I do bind [wearing a tight garment to flatten the chest] when my disabilities allow me to and consider physical transition necessary to be comfortable in myself. The waiting lists are very long – I'm still on the waiting list to see someone to get the dysphoria diagnosed let alone physical transition, and it has had a very big negative effect on my mental health.'

'I'm not interested in physically transition – currently, the way I look works with both more masculine or more feminine ways of presenting and I'm happy with that. I'm not interested in hormones or surgery. Maybe if it was easier to physically transition (both generally, in terms of waiting times, and as a genderqueer person), I would consider it but currently I'm mostly happy as I am. The most physical thing I've done is cut my hair short.'

'Physical transition has enabled me to present my gender how I want to. To be more confident and playful in who I am. To be less scared.'

Legal transition

Some transgender individuals choose to also undertake a legal transition. In the UK, transgender individuals can have their legal gender changed (from one binary gender to the other) under the Gender Recognition Act 2004. They can do this by applying for a Gender Recognition Certificate. In order to do so they must have received a diagnosis of gender dysphoria and have two doctors (their GP and their gender specialist) provide documentation to support this diagnosis. They must also have been living in their 'acquired gender' (i.e. the gender with which they self-identify) for at least two years. If an individual is able to obtain a Gender Recognition Certificate this will change their legal gender and entitle them to a new birth certificate with the correct gender on it. They will also be able to obtain other legal documents, such as passports and driving licences, featuring the correct gender. As with all aspects of transitioning, not all transgender individuals choose to undergo a legal transition. For non-binary people, there is currently no legal option for their gender to be recognised on legal documents such as birth certificates.

Conclusion

Within the trans community, there are a wide range of identities and experiences. While some trans individuals have an experience of transitioning from one binary gender to the other, many have an identity and a transition process which falls outside this binary way of experiencing gender. For all trans people, regardless of their specific gender identity, the process of coming out and transitioning is one that requires a huge amount of both courage and strength. As we will see in the next chapter, while coming out and transitioning are absolutely vital processes for many trans people, the simple fact of living as a trans person can also make one vulnerable to many types of transphobic abuse, violence and discrimination.

Chapter 2
Violence Experienced by the Trans Community

Prevalence, Outcomes and Implications for Service Provision

Introduction

Transgender individuals experience high rates of violence, discrimination and oppression, both at an interpersonal level, through the use for example of physical force and verbal abuse, and at a structural level, in the systematic ways in which social structures harm or otherwise disadvantage them. This chapter will look in detail at these experiences and how they influence the kind of support transgender individuals require following experiences of sexual violence. Particularly, we will explore the short- and long-term consequences for trans individuals living amid this kind of violence and oppression, and how these are intertwined with additional barriers in place for transgender individuals who wish to access support services. This kind of understanding is key in offering good quality support both in terms of overcoming some of these barriers and in being able to deeply connect with trans individuals as clients.

Prevalence

Data on trans experiences of violence is currently limited across the world, as this is territory that research, science and society are only on the cusp of breaching. Here we summarise key findings from the largest UK and US surveys, with the recognition that advocates, researchers and transgender communities will greatly benefit from additional research so that everyone can better understand the lived experiences of trans people around the world.

Nevertheless, the numbers that we do have highlight how violence, oppression and discrimination experienced by transgender individuals are both systemic and personal in nature and occur across the lifespan. Transgender people have these experiences within family environments, educational settings and work environments, and while trying to access housing and medical care. Trans individuals are also susceptible to experiencing violence while interacting with the criminal justice system. In the following pages, we will look more closely at each of these areas in turn.

Experiences of violence in the family

While some trans people experience support and acceptance within their families of origin, others find that their experiences of violence or discrimination begin within them.

In the 2015 *U.S. Transgender Survey*,[4] more than half (60%) of those who were out to their immediate family reported that their family was supportive, while 18 per cent said that they were unsupportive and 22 per cent said that they were neither supportive nor unsupportive (James *et al.* 2016, p.70). Among those who were unsupported by their families, the family's reaction was often violent or extreme: one in ten (10%) of those who were out to their immediate family reported that a family member was violent

---

4   The 2015 *U.S. Transgender Survey* included 27,715 transgender respondents who were living in the US, American Samoa, Guam, Puerto Rico, and US military bases overseas. This study is the largest and most comprehensive study into the lives of transgender individuals in the US to date.

towards them because they were transgender, and 8 per cent were kicked out of the house because they were transgender (James *et al.* 2016, p.2). The report also found that a lack of family support was associated with a host of other negative outcomes and other experiences of violence and oppression for those transgender people who were rejected by their families. These individuals were nearly twice as likely to have experienced homelessness and were 16 per cent more likely to have attempted suicide compared to those who were not rejected by their families (ibid., p.65).

> 'Within an hour of coming out to my parents, I was kicked out into the cold with very few items and my car taken away. I was soon informed by my college that my parents had withdrawn my tuition for the upcoming spring semester. I was devastated.' (James *et al.* 2016, p.68)

> 'My father physically assaulted me and kicked me out of the house. He screamed at me, calling me pathetic, a waste, worthless, and so on. I sat in silence.' (ibid., p.68)

Trans people can benefit greatly from experiencing support within their family. At times, this support is immediate, as described by this transgender individual:

> 'When I finally had the courage to come out, my parents, who I knew would freak out, did the unthinkable. They assured me I had their complete support to be who I am. I was never prouder than in that moment.' (James *et al.* 2016, p.68)

At other times, families take longer to adjust to and accept a new way of understanding and interacting with their transgender family member. Even in these circumstances, their support is valuable:

'It took my family a while to come around. At first they didn't accept me, but they eventually saw how much happier I am and are now my biggest supporters.' (James *et al.* 2016, p.68)

Experiences of violence in education and work

Trans people face a deeply concerning rate of violence and discrimination in education and work, even from a very young age. The 2011 *Injustice at Every Turn* report[5] found that in the US, 'those who expressed a transgender identity or gender non-conformity while in grades K–12 reported alarming rates of harassment (78%), physical assault (35%) and sexual violence (12%)' (Grant *et al.* 2011, p.3). Within work, the level of harassment experienced was even higher as '90% of those surveyed reported experiencing harassment, mistreatment or discrimination on the job or took actions like hiding who they are to avoid it' (Grant *et al.* 2011, p.3). These experiences of discrimination may contribute to the 15 per cent unemployment rate documented in the *2015 U.S. Transgender Survey*, which is three times higher than the unemployment rate in the overall US population at the time of the survey (James *et al.* 2016, p.3). Furthermore, those who experience unemployment are twice as likely to experience homelessness, are 70 per cent more likely to experience incarceration, and have double the HIV (human immunodeficiency virus) infection rate compared to those who are employed (Grant *et al.* 2011, p.3).

In the UK, according to the *Trans Mental Health Study*

---

5 The *Injustice at Every Turn* report (Grant *et al.* 2011) used data from the National Transgender Discrimination Survey, which included responses from 6450 transgender and gender non-conforming individuals from across the US. This was the first comprehensive national transgender discrimination study in the US.

(McNeil *et al.* 2012),[6] 19 per cent of transgender individuals reported experiencing harassment or discrimination at work – still an unacceptably high number (p.70). The same study also found that 52 per cent of the participants had experienced problems with work due to being trans; 18 per cent believed that they had been unfairly turned down for a job; and 16 per cent had not applied for a job due to fear of harassment and discrimination (McNeil *et al.* 2012, p.70).

Struggles with discrimination, violence or unemployment can lead transgender individuals into sex work when they might not otherwise have chosen this line of work (Sausa, Keatley and Operario 2007). For some, sex work is the only viable way of earning a living. One 2006 study about the lives of gender-variant and transgender people in Argentina found that among the 257 respondents, 84.2 per cent earned their living by doing sex work and 77.5 per cent of those said they would quit doing sex work if they could (Instituto Runa 2007, cited in Balzer and Hutta 2012, p.47). For many transgender sex workers, their gender identity makes them particularly vulnerable to violence. The *2015 U.S. Transgender Survey* found that among those who were working in the underground economy (including in sex work) at the time of taking the survey, 41 per cent had experienced a physical attack in the last year and 36 per cent had been sexually assaulted during the past year (James *et al.* 2016, p.12). Similarly, in their worldwide comparative review, Balzer and Hutta (2012) report that sex workers are particularly vulnerable to insults, physical abuse, rape and murder in many parts of the world. For example, in Central and South America

---

6   This is the most comprehensive UK and Ireland study to date. It was undertaken by the Scottish Transgender Alliance and published in 2012. The study included 889 transgender and gender non-conforming individuals living in the UK and Ireland.

78 per cent of trans murder victims whose profession was reported (258 out of 643 murders) were sex workers.

These difficulties in securing and maintaining safe employment result in high levels of poverty among transgender individuals. The *2015 U.S. Transgender Survey* found that nearly one-third (29%) of respondents were living in poverty, compared to 14 per cent in the US population (James *et al.* 2016, p.3). An earlier study found that transgender individuals were four times as likely to have an income under $10,000 compared to the overall US population (Grant *et al.* 2011, p.2). In a pan-European study, respondents reported salary levels which were disproportionately at the lower end, with 37.4 per cent earning under €20,000 per year (Whittle *et al.* 2008, p.47).

Experiences of violence in housing

Transgender individuals experience significant discrimination too when attempting to access housing. The difficulties faced by transgender people in finding and maintaining stable work makes it more difficult to access the private rented sector, where prices are often high, or to obtain a mortgage. Some also face landlords who are unwilling to let out homes to transgender people. The *2015 U.S. Transgender Survey* found that 6 per cent of transgender respondents had been refused a house or apartment because they were transgender, with significantly more trans women of colour experiencing this (11–15%) (James *et al.* 2016, p.179), thus showing the compounding effects of ethnicity and gender identity. Moreover, transgender individuals who have been rejected by their family do not have the vital safety net of family-provided accommodation or help with funding their own accommodation.

Given the difficulties in securing stable housing as outlined above, it is not surprising that the homelessness rates among transgender individuals are shockingly high. In the UK, the *Trans Mental Health Study* found that 19 per cent of respondents had been homeless at some point, with 11 per cent having been homeless more than once (McNeil *et al.* 2012, p.71). In the 2015 *U.S. Transgender Survey*, 30 per cent of respondents said that they experienced homelessness at some point in their lifetime and 12 per cent said that they experienced homelessness within the past year (James *et al.* 2016, p.3).

When attempting to access crisis housing services, transgender individuals can face difficulties if housing options are gendered. Such services may be less willing to support transgender individuals, and transgender people may feel less safe accessing binary-gendered services. This same dilemma creates difficulties for transgender individuals of all genders if they need to access refuge accommodation while fleeing domestic violence. Moreover, utilising such services can prove dangerous due to the risk of harassment or assault. Grant and colleagues (2011) report that when attempting to access homeless shelters, 55 per cent of transgender individuals were harassed by shelter staff or residents, 29 per cent were turned away and 22 per cent reported being sexually assaulted by residents or staff (p.4). The 2015 *U.S. Transgender Survey* found that 'seven out of ten respondents who stayed at a shelter in the past year faced some form of mistreatment, such as being forced out, harassed, or attacked because of being transgender' (James *et al.* 2016, p.181). One respondent of that study reported, 'When I go to shelters, I am admonished and told that I should return to "being a woman" in order to use the shelter system' (James *et al.* 2016, p.179).

Experiences of violence in healthcare

Accessing healthcare is another area in which transgender people can face discrimination and violence. Many find themselves needing to educate ill-informed medical professionals or are asked inappropriate and unnecessary questions.

In relation to transition-related healthcare, many US transgender individuals find that their health insurance is unwilling to cover medical procedures related to their transition. In the US, James and colleagues (2016) found that 55 per cent of survey respondents reported that their insurance was unwilling to cover transition-related surgery. Twenty-five per cent said their insurance was unwilling to cover their hormone treatment. Respondents also reported their insurance declining to cover a variety of other procedures, including 15 per cent reporting that they were able to access services traditionally thought of as gender-specific such as cervical or prostate examinations, and 7 per cent reported that they were denied other routine healthcare (James *et al.* 2016, p.95).

Issues of access to necessary transition-related care are not unique to the United States. For instance, while transgender individuals in the UK do not face the same problems posed by many US health insurance companies, many people still face tremendous difficulty in accessing appropriate care in a timely manner via the NHS. In the UK, most transgender individuals who wish to receive transition-related healthcare via the NHS are referred to a gender identity clinic (GIC). There can be long waits for initial appointments at GICs, followed by further waits for treatments such as hormones, various surgeries and voice training. These long waits can cause enormous distress. As one respondent to the *Trans Mental Health Study* put it, 'it's like you are waiting for permission to live' (McNeil *et al.* 2012, p.59). After the long wait for an initial appointment, 46 per cent of the participants in the above study reported problems accessing the gender-related treatment they needed. These problems stemmed from a range of issues including 'administrative errors, restrictive protocols, problematic attitudes, and unnecessary questions or tests' (McNeil *et al.* 2012, pp.28–29). When accessing healthcare outside a GIC, over 60 per cent felt that they had to educate a health worker, and over 50 per cent were told that the professional did not know enough about trans health-care to provide it, while in nearly 30 per cent of cases, a healthcare professional had refused to discuss a trans-related health concern (McNeil *et al.* 2012, p.45).

Trans voices

'Since I transitioned ten years ago, I have experienced constant, systematic administrative violence and discrim-ination at the hands of the NHS, particularly at primary care level. Many GPs I've seen haven't known how to treat me, and some haven't wanted to treat me. Some have refused to give me eye contact and empathy, making the appointments more about sympathising with "what I've done to my mum" rather than providing healthcare. Some appear embarrassed and flustered in their lack of knowledge on the correct terminology for my gender, body, treatments and trans healthcare in general. Some have refused to provide my testosterone injections even though I was prescribed them ten years ago and haven't been told to stop by the GIC. Some have refused smear tests and ultrasounds even though the GIC recommends trans men undergo these every couple of years. Some have refused to refer me for the revision surgery I need; some write the referrals but write them incorrectly or send them to the wrong commissioning body – and won't listen when I try to correct them.

'Generally, many GPs seem to have little knowledge of the current NHS GIC protocol and many do not read the copies of the protocol and best practice guidelines that I provide to them. Their lack of knowledge of the protocol, and of how detrimental non-clinical delay is for trans people, has a widely, deeply detrimental effect on the healthcare I receive, and on my state of health more generally. I am chronically, severely mentally ill and have told almost all my GPs that they are responsible for that, as I believe if they successfully referred me for the revision surgery I need when I first needed it, seven years ago, I would not have become as ill as I am now.'

While little research on transition-related care has so far been conducted in other countries, in a Europe-wide study, Whittle and colleagues (2008)[7] found that:

More than half of the groups at both ends of our occupational and earnings spectrum are paying for surgery themselves after being refused State funding. Given that nearly half of all respondents are in the lower income bracket of less than €25,000 per year this is an onerous and unnecessary financial burden. (Whittle *et al.* 2008, p.11)

In April 2017, there were still 22 countries in Europe where transgender individuals are required to undergo surgical sterilisation

---

7   The 2008 Transgender Euro Study included a survey of 1964 transgender individuals across Europe.

before they can legally have their gender recognised (Transgender Europe 2017). As such, many individuals are forced to have an unwanted and unnecessary major operation in order to obtain legal recognition of their gender. There is hope that many of the countries will change these laws, as in its judgement of the complaint A.P., Garçon and Nicot v France in 2017 (application nos. 79885/12, 52471/13 and 52596/13), the European Court of Human Rights determined that the requirement to undergo sterilisation violates human rights.

Trans people can also experience discrimination when accessing primary care that is not related to their trans status. The *2015 U.S. Transgender Survey* found that among those trans respondents who had accessed healthcare in the US over the past year, 15 per cent reported being asked intrusive or unnecessary questions about their gender which were not relevant to the presenting health concern (p.95). Importantly, this report also found that, 'nearly one-quarter (23%) of respondents reported that at some point in the past year they needed health care but did not seek it due to fear of being disrespected or mistreated as a transgender person' (James *et al.* 2016, p.98). Such discrimination included misgendering, refusing to accept a patient's gender identity and making jokes about the patient. These experiences cause significant pain and can make it less likely for patients to access care in the future.

'Multiple medical professionals have misgendered me, denied to me that I was transgender or tried to persuade me that my trans identity was just a misdiagnosis of something else, have made jokes at my expense in front of me and behind my back, and have made me feel physically unsafe. I often do not seek medical attention when it is needed, because I'm afraid of what harassment or discrimination I may experience in a hospital or clinic.' (James *et al.* 2016, p.96)

Experiences of violence within the criminal justice system

In instances when transgender people interact with the criminal justice system (CJS), they are once again vulnerable to discrimination and abuse. The 2015 *U.S. Transgender Survey* reported that 58 per cent of respondents who had interacted with police or law enforcement officers over the past year experienced some form of mistreatment during this interaction, including harassment, refusal to use the correct gender/pronoun when referring to the transgender person, physical assault or sexual assault (James *et al.* 2016, p.12). Physical violence perpetrated by law enforcement officers is also documented in many nations. For example, the Transrespect vs Transphobia[8] report references video evidence of the execution of three transgender individuals by the police in Iraq (Balzer and Hutta 2012, p.39).

Another survey reports that, as a result of CJS-related violence, 46 per cent of transgender people were uncomfortable seeking police assistance (Grant *et al.* 2011, p.5). Transgender individuals in many European nations report a similar lack of confidence in the police, with one report noting that 85 per cent of respondents in Greece expressed this lack of confidence, followed by 68 per cent in Hungary, 54 per cent in Italy and 51 per cent in France (Turner, Whittle and Combs 2009, p.24).[9]

---

8   In 2012, Transrespect vs Transphobia Worldwide produced *A Comparative Review of the Human-rights Situation of Gender-variant/Trans People,* which is the most comprehensive research report to date on the human rights situation of trans and gender-variant people around the world.

9   The *Transphobic Hate Crime in the European Union* report (Turner, Whittle and Combs 2009) gives important insight into the violence faced by transgender individuals in the European Union (EU). This study included 2669 gender-variant and/or trans people who responded to the study in 13 languages across all EU member states.

Imprisoned transgender people can also face appalling conditions. Frequently reported problems include transgender individuals being imprisoned in prisons which house the wrong gender (for example, a trans woman being housed in a men's prison), and being kept in solitary confinement 'for their own safety', or being denied the ability to dress in accordance with their gender identity, facing increased rates of sexual assault in prison and being refused gender-related healthcare (Center for American Progress and MAP 2016).

In the UK, there have been several recent media stories about trans people who have committed suicide while in prison. For example, in December 2016, Jenny Swift, a trans woman, was found dead in her cell at the all-male prison where she had been living for five weeks. It was also reported that she had been refused female hormones while in prison (Halliday 2017).

Sexual violence, domestic violence and hate crime

In addition to the systemic oppression and violence highlighted above, transgender individuals also experience heightened levels of interpersonal violence and hate crime. Experiences of domestic violence and sexual violence are unacceptably high among transgender people, with 54 per cent reporting having experienced some form of intimate partner violence and 47 per cent reporting that they have been sexually assaulted at some point in their lives (James *et al.* 2016, p.13). Experiences of sexual assault are even more common among trans people in sex work (72%), those who have experienced homelessness (65%), and those with disabilities (61%) (ibid.).

Transgender individuals are also vulnerable to hate crimes, including transphobic murders. The Trans Murder Monitoring

Project attempts to track and report on such murders, although their statistics are likely to only capture a small portion of the transphobic murders which occur each year, due to a lack of any central reporting mechanisms and the problem of unreported murders. As of 31 March 2017, they had recorded and reported on the murders of 2343 transgender individuals over a nine-year period (TvT research project 2015).

Trans voices

'I was sexually assaulted by an ex-partner after I disclosed my trans status; they were of the opinion that sex would make me see myself as a girl. I have also been physically assaulted by people in my school and by a stranger in a bathroom.'

Intersectional experiences of oppression and violence

The experiences of discrimination, oppression and violence of transgender people who have more than one marginalised identity are often particularly pronounced and extreme. As reported in the *2015 U.S. Transgender Survey* (James *et al.* 2016, p.4), transgender individuals with disabilities also face very high levels of discrimination and violence. According to the same survey, the unemployment rate among disabled respondents was 24 per cent, and 45 per cent of disabled respondents were living in poverty. Additionally, these respondents reported high levels of psychological distress (59%) and 54 per cent reported that they had attempted suicide in their lifetime. Many had very negative experiences of care provision too, with 42 per cent reporting that they had been mistreated by healthcare providers.

The authors also report that transgender people of colour experience deeper and broader patterns of discrimination than white respondents and the US population as a whole. Compared to their white counterparts, trans people of colour, including Latino/a (43%), American Indian (41%), multiracial (40%), and black (38%) respondents, were up to three times as likely as the US population (14%) to be living in poverty. The unemployment rate among transgender people of colour was 20 per cent, four times higher than the US unemployment rate (5%). This report also noted that undocumented immigrants faced significantly heightened levels of both economic hardship and violence. In the year prior to the survey, 24 per cent of undocumented immigrant respondents reported having been physically attacked. Half reported experiencing homelessness at some point in their lifetime and 68 per cent reported experiencing intimate partner violence (James *et al.* 2016, p.4).

Impact on well-being: mental health and suicide

Unsurprisingly, the violence, abuse and discrimination described in this chapter have a catastrophic effect on the emotional, physical, economic and social well-being of many trans individuals. Around the world, trans individuals face daily battles for their safety, to be recognised as who they are and to receive the care and support they need. This battle takes its toll and many people report high levels of emotional distress, physical illness/disability and difficult material circumstances.

The *Trans Mental Health Survey* also documented high rates of various types of mental ill-health among trans individuals. Eighty-eight per cent of respondents reported that they were currently experiencing or had previously experienced depression; 75 per cent reported the same about anxiety (McNeil *et al.* 2012, p.50). More than half of respondents (58%) reported that at some point they had felt so distressed that they needed to urgently seek help, but 35 per cent of these individuals avoided seeking this help because of their trans identity (ibid., p.52).

The cumulative effect of this is that many transgender individuals come to experience life as simply unlivable in their current circumstances. As a result, the rate of suicide attempts among the trans population is very high. In the US, 40 per cent of respondents to the *U.S. Transgender Survey* reported that they had attempted suicide at some point in their lifetime, and a heartbreaking 82 per cent of respondents had seriously considered ending their own lives at some point (James *et al.* 2016, p.114). Another survey found that among transgender individuals who had survived sexual assault, 64 per cent had attempted suicide at some point in their lives (Grant *et al.* 2011, p.2). In the UK, 35 per cent of transgender individuals who took part in the *Trans Mental Health Study* reported that they had attempted suicide at least once in their lifetime, and 89 per cent reported having seriously considered ending their life (McNeil *et al.* 2012, p.59). Across Europe, the rate of attempted suicide among transgender individuals is only slightly lower, 29.9 per cent (Whittle *et al.* 2008, p.49).

Risk and protective factors for reducing the impact of violence

Despite these high levels of discrimination and disadvantage, trans individuals and communities around the world have found ways to survive and indeed thrive. Many find strength within both themselves and their communities.

Individual protective factors

In order to live well in the face of all the violence described above, many trans people must find inner resources that help them to understand, cope with and challenge the difficulties they have faced. Singh, Hays and Watson (2011) have found four individual characteristics which contribute to resilience among trans people. First among these is an 'evolving and self-generated definition of self' (p.23). This entails an ability to define for oneself key parts of one's identity, including one's gender identity. Second is the ability to embrace self-worth and third is an awareness of the level of oppression faced by transgender people. These three qualities can help trans people to maintain a strong belief in their own value despite the many negative messages they receive from society about themselves. Finally, the authors found that cultivating hope for their futures is another key aspect of personal resilience in trans people.

The role of community support

It is widely understood that being part of a supportive community of other transgender people is hugely valuable in promoting the resilience of trans people (Bariola *et al.* 2015; Bockting *et al.* 2013; Singh *et al.* 2011). When rejected from their birth families or previous communities, trans people find chosen families which can offer them support and community. Faced with insurance companies or national health services that are unwilling to pay for necessary treatment, transgender individuals often seek and find financial support from other members of the trans community and their allies.

Having experienced acts of hate and violence, people come together to find ways to heal and even to educate others so as to prevent further such acts of hate. When denied opportunities for paid employment, many transgender people find opportunities to contribute to their community and enrich their own skill sets, often through volunteering or activism within the trans community. Simply being part of a community of people who deeply understand your own experiences can be extremely valuable.

This resilience, in the most difficult of circumstances, is an incredible resource and strength within the transgender community. All transgender people deserve a world in which they no longer face discrimination or violence because of their gender; they also deserve to be recognised for the incredible strength and resilience required to keep surviving and thriving in the world as it is today.

Trans voices

'I came out to my family age 18. My mum ignored what I had said and later made it about her – worries about what the neighbours would think of her, whether she'd get any grandchildren and so on. I asked her not to tell my stepdad as he had been physically and emotionally abusive to me since I was a child. She told him anyway. He was being very aggressive, shouting and banging his fists on the table while making various transphobic comments. He asked some questions about transition but didn't like my answers – he didn't seem to want me to have any answers, so as to more easily persuade me against transition. He then became physically violent, hitting me and pushing me against the wall. He sexually assaulted me to "prove" I was a girl, and then told me to leave and never come back. I managed to pack a few things and then left. I sofa-surfed and slept rough for a few months and was then offered a place in a hostel. My room had no running water, no appliances, no lights, and had infestations. The hostel was far out of town and I didn't have any money to get the bus, so I couldn't get out to see friends, or to the Job Centre 12 miles away. Therefore, I couldn't claim any benefits to buy food or pay the bills, which put me in debt.

'Sometimes I would try to walk back to my hometown so I could eat at friends' houses. On one occasion, I sat outside near to my family home and they just walked past me, shielding my sister from me because I looked quite ill. By the end of that period of my life I had lost around half my body weight and was experiencing psychosis, starvation and isolation – I was just stuck, with nothing and no one, and dealing with gender dysphoria on top of it. I had to go to hospital due to the effects of having no food, and am still in therapy due to the emotional effects the experience had on me. What my parents put me through for being trans has changed me as a person and will probably affect my well-being forever. But I had little choice: if I hadn't come out at the time, I would have killed myself; I couldn't cope in that body any longer.

'Later that year I was able to get in touch with an old friend who came to where I was staying, and we went to the library to use the computers. We found that I had been accepted onto a university course – in focusing on basic survival, I had completely forgotten that I had applied. She lent me some money so I could get the train to uni, 200 miles away. I was scared to leave everything that was familiar, but knew I wasn't welcome there anymore, so I packed all my things and got on the train. I had no idea where I was going or where I would sleep that night; I knew it was risky. But when I arrived the receptionist was really kind and found me a room. Various administrative staff and lecturers looked after me in my first year; they helped me to sort out my university fees and bursaries and helped me to settle in. I quickly made friends on my course and through the LGBT Society, and soon enough I joined the LGBT Society committee and started to volunteer at various trans organisations and social groups in the city. Ten years later I am still friends with many of the LGBT people who accepted me then, and I think my life would have been a lot harder without the community.'

Implications for service provision

There is no doubt that transgender individuals continue to face profound discrimination and violence and that all of this impacts on their well-being in profoundly negative ways. These experiences also have implications for the service providers who aim to support transgender individuals.

It is essential for service providers to hold in mind that transgender service users will likely experience discrimination and a lack of safety (both physical and emotional) as a part of their daily lives. Given this, it is entirely reasonable for transgender individuals to assume that any environment and indeed any person may be unsafe or harmful until proven otherwise. Their previous (and indeed current) experiences may make them hesitant to access services out of fear that they will once again experience discrimination, violence or abuse at the hands of you or your organisation. It is up to us, as service providers, to gently, continually and persistently demonstrate the safety of our services.

In the next chapter, we will look more deeply at the impact of trauma, particularly trauma that has resulted from experiences of sexual violence. This will give further insight into the impact of violence and discrimination on the lives of transgender individuals, including at the neurological level.

Chapter 3
Trauma and Its Effects

Introduction

In the last three decades, a large body of evidence-based knowledge has accumulated about the effects of overwhelming stress. As our understanding grows about the complex nature and impact of overwhelming experiences, we are recognising that sexual violence is often traumatic, affecting the individual's physical, emotional, spiritual and relational well-being. This chapter offers a broad overview of how sexual trauma impacts survivors and what makes sexual violence traumatic in the first place. This knowledge can directly inform how we can best support survivors in managing the aftermath of the violence and regaining control over their lives. It can also help us address many heartbreakingly common misconceptions about an individual's experience of sexual violence and their response to it. The remainder of the chapter will explore the highly complex and individualised responses to sexual trauma, and what may be the personal and social factors involved in these differences. First, however, let us turn to what trauma actually is.

What do we mean by trauma?

Trauma literally means 'wound', from the Greek τραύμα. While the term was originally coined to describe bodily injuries, in this context it refers to invisible wounds in the psyche. Psychological wounds can be as painful as (if not more painful than) physical injuries, but they are more difficult to identify because they can only be known by the telling of one's story. More commonly, they manifest through a wide range of symptoms which indicate a difficulty in coping or functioning normally following the traumatic experience.

Psychological trauma stems from events that are *perceived* to pose a serious threat to one's life and well-being. These events include one-time incidents, like flooding, earthquakes and car accidents, and repetitive events, such as war, concentration camps and domestic abuse. The word *perceived* is key as it reflects the subjective component in what makes an event traumatic for one person, but not for the other. In other words, it is not for *us* to determine whether a particular event is traumatic; that is up to each survivor. However, traumatic events often share common characteristics, such as the abuse of power and the betrayal of trust, coupled with a sense of helplessness, confusion and loss by the person who experiences them. Traumatic events also often impact the entire person; the way we think, the way we learn, the way we remember things, the way we feel about ourselves, the way we feel about other people, and the way we make sense of the world are all profoundly altered by those experiences. It is very normal for people to experience reactions such as repeated strong and fragmented memories of the traumatic event(s), feelings of shock, confusion, fear, anxiety and numbness. These reactions may be experienced days, months or years after the trauma and may last for a few days or weeks, or for a longer time.

Experiences of sexual violence are often traumatic events because they display most if not all of these characteristics. As with other traumas, sexual trauma can stem from a one-off event, such as date rape, or multiple, repeated occurrences as in the case of sexual violence within a relationship. In line with the definition of trauma, sexual violence survivors often recount experiencing physical and emotional violation. This violation can be acted through physical force or, more often, through psychological coercion, for example someone using authority over them (such as a doctor, teacher or parent), being bribed or manipulated, being threatened with assault (or that people they care about will be hurt if they do not comply), or not being able to give consent (if asleep or too intoxicated). Similar to other traumatic experiences, sexual violence often produces short-term and long-term physical consequences. It is normal for survivors to experience feelings of intense fear, powerlessness, hopelessness and other trauma-reaction symptoms in the aftermath of sexual violence. The world doesn't feel like a safe place anymore. There is no longer trust in others or even themselves. Survivors may question their judgement, their self-worth and even their sanity. Some survivors experience a reduction in symptoms within a few months, whereas some experience distress for years. Long-term outcomes include post-traumatic stress disorder (PTSD), depression, eating disorders, sexual dysfunction, alcohol and illicit drug use, non-fatal suicidal behaviour and suicidal threats, physical symptoms in the absence of medical conditions, and severe preoccupations with physical appearances.

To understand why sexual trauma can have such a damaging and lasting impact on one's entire person, it's important to understand the way the brain is wired to respond to trauma. The brain's response to trauma is complex, and human behaviour in response to trauma, particularly sexual violence, is not well understood, although recent research does offer some important insights.

Trauma and the brain

Many people will be familiar with the experience of instinctively reacting to a threat. For example, let us imagine that we are walking in the woods, when suddenly we encounter something curly and black on our path: in all probability, our first reaction is to stop on the spot. This reaction is outside our conscious control: we freeze whether what is actually in front of us is a snake or a piece of rubber that we mistake for a snake. Only a few seconds later, our conscious brain catches up and is able to process whether the danger is real (a snake) or perceived (a piece of rubber). This is because humans process danger through the 'instinctive' part of their brain, which they share with all other vertebrates. This part is responsible for automatic body processes and it is older, in evolutionary terms, than our 'thinking brain', which is responsible for analytical thinking and other conscious processes. This 'instinctive' brain can make us fight the danger or run away ('flight'). Another common reaction, as in the above example of the snake, is to 'freeze'. In these instances, we become still, as if we are riveted to the spot, breathing shallowly or holding our breath altogether: the phrases 'scared stiff' or 'frozen with fear' represent this response.

Unlike what our 'thinking' brain would like us to believe, when faced with serious threats most humans do not fight or run away. The instinctive part of the brain over thousands of years has learned that our best chance is often to freeze, as we are weaker and slower than our natural predators. The duration of this freeze response may vary until such a time when fighting back or running away become possible, or until the danger subsides. If you have seen any of those nature documentaries you might have noticed how animals like gazelles will lie motionless if they sense a predator is nearby, in the hope of avoiding being tracked.

Going back to the snake example, the instinctive brain will have processed the snake-like features of the piece of rubber in the woods and activated a freeze response before the thinking brain, which is capable of logical thought, is able to process it as a piece of rubber. At that point, we can relax and maybe think, 'silly me, it's just a piece of rubber'. Processing danger in this way is very efficient, because it means that we do not even need to think before we act to protect ourselves when we feel threatened or injured. In other words, our brain prioritises survival above anything else: after all, reflecting on our experience or the longer-term consequences of our actions is not much use when we may be mortally bitten by a snake (see the section below for further details on the neuroscience of trauma).

How does the way our brain responds to trauma apply to, say, sexual assault? In this case, the instinctive brain is likely to reject screaming, running or fight, because these are more likely to increase the risk of serious injury: we may get restrained, silenced, beaten into submission. So, we are likely to freeze. This explains the reaction of many victims of sexual violence, who report feeling as if they could not escape, even when no weapon was present. In sexual assault, the freezing response is ignored by the perpetrator, so as the assault continues, the victim's muscles may instinctively relax in order to yield to any physical impact ('flop'), and the victim may become dissociative – they may mentally escape as physical escape is not an option. Dissociating often results in memories of the event being fragmented later on, and chunks blacked out, which means that an individual can fail to correctly encode and store memories experienced during trauma, as neuroimaging research shows (Kolk, Burbridge and Suzuki 1997). Conversely, what is most likely to get encoded into memory tends to be powerful and fragmentary sensations, images and feelings, which do not just 'go away' once the danger has passed. They are deeply imprinted and even when the danger has ceased it can take a while to once again feel safe, as if our alarm system is now always activated. These advances in our understanding of the altered functioning of the brain in traumatic situations should make it unreasonable to expect a trauma survivor to recall traumatic events the way they would recall, say, their last holiday. Yet, ignorance around how trauma impacts memory can lead to misinterpreting the discrepancies in survivors' stories as lies, rather than as their brain's response to extreme trauma.

The role of the instinctive brain to keep us alive is also linked to the extent to which the brain successfully maintains attachments. Survival and attachments are inextricably intertwined: as humans, we are born totally dependent on our adult caregivers for all our survival needs. This attachment is the foundation for our future psychological, emotional, physical and mental development as well as the template for all future relationships with others. It also implies that when we are in great danger, unlike non-social species that may seek safety in a place, as humans we have a biological drive to find safety in one another and, particularly, to seek proximity with our attachment figure. For example, in the immediate aftermath of the 9/11 attacks, many people in close proximity sought to re-establish contact with loved ones rather than fleeing the scene (Schein 2006).

This has implications for those who have experienced sexual violence by someone they are particularly attached to, such as an abusive partner or parent, as most people will respond by ensuring that the attachment to that person is continued, despite the abuse. Hence, even if escape is objectively possible, their reaction will rarely be one of fight or flight, keeping them vulnerable to repeated abuse.

The neuroscience of trauma

Let us understand in greater detail the biological basis for the way our brain responds when we encounter a dangerous situation.

To gain a deeper understanding of the brain response when we encounter a dangerous situation, we can look at the brain in terms of its evolutionary history. The triune brain model, introduced by the American scientist Paul D MacLean (1990), describes the brain as made of three complexes emerging successively along an evolutionary path (Figure 3.1). With reference to this model, what we have called the instinctive brain can actually be seen as compromising two parts: the 'reptilian complex', which is the oldest part in the brain and controls the body's vital functions such as heart rate, breathing, body temperature and balance; and the 'limbic system', which is responsible for assigning emotional valence to our experiences, and which plays an essential part in activating threat responses and in learning and memory formation.

Last to develop in evolutionary terms is what we called the 'thinking brain', which is mainly associated with the neocortex, a structure only found in higher mammals, and which is responsible for the higher-order abilities of our species such as language, abstract thought and planning (Figure 3.1).

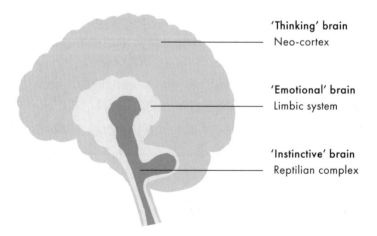

'Thinking' brain
Neo-cortex

'Emotional' brain
Limbic system

'Instinctive' brain
Reptilian complex

Figure 3.1: *A schematic representation of the triune brain model (adapted from MacLean 1990)*

The instinctive and thinking brain do not operate independently of one another. They have established numerous interconnections through which they influence one another.

For example, every piece of sensory input that enters our brain in the reptilian complex via the thalamus (the relay station of the brain) is then sent to the limbic system (short route) and, in particular, a structure called the amygdala, while a much slower signal sends the same information to the neocortex for further evaluation (long route).

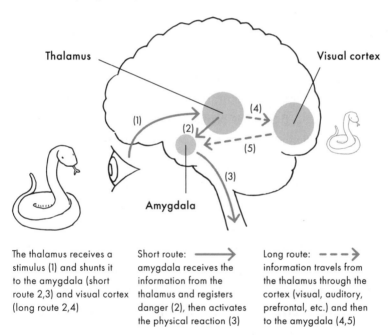

The thalamus receives a stimulus (1) and shunts it to the amygdala (short route 2,3) and visual cortex (long route 2,4)

Short route: ⟶ amygdala receives the information from the thalamus and registers danger (2), then activates the physical reaction (3)

Long route: ⇢ information travels from the thalamus through the cortex (visual, auditory, prefrontal, etc.) and then to the amygdala (4,5)

Figure 3.2: *Illustration of the brain's natural response to threat and danger*

As with all sensory information, when confronted with perceived or actual danger (see Figure 3.2), the sensory input is received first by the thalamus. The thalamus then sends signals directly to the amygdala via the short route, while also signalling to the cortex to evaluate the situation. The amygdala is therefore able to process sensory information and initiate a behavioural response (fight or flight) *before* the information reaches the cortex for further elaboration.

When our fight-or-flight response is activated by the amygdala, sequences of nerve cell firing occur and chemicals like adrenaline, noradrenaline and cortisol are released into our bloodstream, causing a series of dramatic changes in our body. Blood is directed away from our digestive system into our muscles, which require extra energy and fuel for running and fighting. Our pupils dilate. Our awareness intensifies. Our sight sharpens. Our impulses quicken. Our perception of pain diminishes. We become prepared – physically and psychologically – for fight or flight. If the danger persists, the amygdala will deem that fight or flight is not likely to be successful, and thus will alert the freeze response. Often at this point the individual will also begin to dissociate: they will go numb and disengage while in danger, thus mentally escaping a situation where physical escape is no longer possible. In this passive state, the brain releases natural opiates (endorphins) as an analgesic, helping to numb the emotional and physical pain.

By bypassing the higher-processing activities of the neocortex, the short route for amygdala activation allows us to prepare for potential danger before knowing exactly what the danger is. After all, 'better to be wrong and alive, than right and dead' (Ungar 2012, p.115).

The impact of sexual trauma

After a traumatic event, it is typical to have feelings of anxiety, stress or fear, making it difficult to adjust or cope for some time afterwards. In the period just after a sexual trauma, many survivors report feeling shock, confusion, anxiety or numbness. Sometimes they may be in denial, and may not fully accept what has happened to them or downplay the intensity of the experience. In the first few days and weeks following the assault, it is very normal for an individual to experience intense and sometimes unpredictable emotions. Flashbacks, nightmares and intrusive memories are extremely common, especially in the first few months following the assault. For those who develop PTSD,[10] they can last much longer.

A trauma-informed understanding of sexual violence can help us comprehend such reactions. For example, hyper-arousal, a state of heightened sensitivity to external stimuli and events, is directly linked to our instinctive brain being 'stuck' in constant alert. In this state, stress hormones inflame the amygdala (increasing the intensity of sadness, fear and anger) and impair the hippocampal area responsible for memory processing. If these chemicals continue for any length of time the hippocampus shrinks and the amygdala enlarges, thus perpetuating a stress response long after a trauma is over. In other words, even though real danger may not be present, our body acts as if it is, causing lasting stress after a traumatic event, which can impact our ability to function on a daily basis. Symptoms of hyper-arousal may include sleeping problems, difficulties concentrating, irritability, angry outbursts, panic, constant anxiety and intense fear. These symptoms can be difficult to manage, and some survivors may turn to substances like alcohol and drugs, or to self-harm, in an effort to cope with them.

---

10 Some authors (for example, Wasco 2003) are critical of PTSD as a concept, given that, as a psychiatric diagnosis, it medicalises the individual survivor. Also, the symptoms included in the diagnosis of PTSD do not include all the effects that sexual trauma has on individuals. PTSD is criticised too for seeing the event of rape as the cause of trauma, thereby not fully accounting for the gendered and cultured context in which rape occurs (Wasco 2003).

Hyper-arousal symptoms are typically accompanied by flash-backs, which are intrusive and distressing memories of the trauma as if they were happening in the here and now. Some research suggests that the impact of trauma on memory mechanisms underlies flashbacks and the ease with which they are triggered (Ehlers 2010). As the traumatic experience may have several distinct parts that are not necessarily remembered as one integrated event, vivid sensory impressions such as images, sounds, body sensations, tastes or smells experienced during the trauma may act as sensory 'hooks': for example, if during the assault the assailant wore a perfume, and there was music on in the background, the next time we smell a similar perfume, or we hear that music, our mind would go to find a memory associated with those things (much like smelling suncream evokes memories of a great holiday), and the first thing it might come across is the 'unfiled' event (the trauma). As this hasn't been filed away properly, our brain assumes it is a real-life event happening now – it can't distinguish between the unprocessed memory and the present moment.

In this flashback state, the extreme feelings and body sensations occurring are frightening because they are not related to the reality of the present and often seem to come from nowhere. Because people are often not aware of their triggers, flashbacks can be incredibly disruptive and unpredictable events that are difficult to manage. We may begin to think we are crazy and are afraid of telling anyone about what is happening. We feel out of control and at the mercy of our experiences. Fragmented memories can also re-emerge during sleep through nightmares, and survivors may develop insomnia as a way of coping with such dreams.

In an effort to avoid painful memories and feelings associated with the trauma, survivors may try to distance themselves from any possible reminders of the traumatic event, including emotional and social distancing. Emotional avoidance is when a person avoids thoughts or feelings about a traumatic event. For example, rape survivors may try to think about other things whenever thoughts about the rape arise. They might go out of their way to stay away from the scene of their attack, or to avoid people who remind them of the trauma.

Social avoidance can also be linked to feeling different and disconnected from other people. Distrust may also set in, especially if the sexual abuse was perpetrated by someone close to the survivor: if someone who was supposed to love them or protect them could harm them so badly, who can they actually believe and open up to? There may be anger towards the abuser or those who knew and did nothing to protect them. More often than not, however, survivors turn such anger inward; they think that they should have prevented or stopped the abuse. Taking responsibility for the abuse can also be a way to make them feel safe and in control – if only they wear the right clothes or do the right things they can stop it from happening again. It is easier too to blame themselves than think the unthinkable: that someone who loved them could also abuse them. Additionally, other people may encourage the survivor to turn these feelings against themselves, as a way to protect the abuser and/or to make them feel safe – nobody wants it to be true, so it is easier to blame the survivor for lying or for 'asking for it'. In reality, of course, the survivor is never responsible for the sexual violence they suffered; only the perpetrator is.

Sexual trauma can also impact intimacy with others. Survivors' relationships may be affected by their intense emotions, both because they may not have learned how to regulate their emotions and because the trauma may have biologically altered their stress reactions in a way that makes their emotions stronger than usual, making it easier for the instinctive brain to take over. It may be frightening to get back in touch with their body and be sexually intimate with people. Sexual trauma can make them feel as if their body is the enemy, something that's been violated and contaminated – something they may hate or want to ignore. For childhood sexual abuse survivors, their first sexual experiences of arousal may be linked with shame, disgust, pain and humiliation, and they may have internalised the belief that sexual desire is scary, painful and out of their control. Alternatively, others may become promiscuous, believing that they are only good or loved for sex. For others still, being sexual can become a way to claim back their bodies.

Trans voices

'My childhood memories are filled with embarrassing moments, like being forced to use the wrong bathroom at swimming lessons, or having to undress in front of other children. In adolescence, I started to present myself as female, but I still showed obvious remnants of my assigned gender. I hated my body even more after two schoolmates sexually abused me. They were "getting one over" on me because "they could tell" I wasn't a real woman. For a long time after that I experienced dissociation from and hatred towards my body, especially my genitals. It is really hard to "reclaim" your body or parts of it, if you feel it is not yours in the first place. This is even harder if the violence is normalised by transphobic attitudes also viewing the body as "wrong", to the extent that it is understood as not being "real" violence. I think after a time I started to have lots of sex. I just wanted to get myself back, to stop having people asking if I was "okay" because I was a rape survivor.'

Healing from sexual trauma

It is important to note that there is no single response to sexual trauma. Reactions can be immediate or delayed, even after years; some people heal quickly, while others take a long time. How sexual trauma affects an individual depends on many factors, including the individual, the type and characteristics of the violence that has been experienced, and the response of family, friends and the community, to name a few. But with the right strategies and support, survivors can move past the trauma, rebuild their sense of control and self-worth, and come out the other side feeling stronger and more resilient.

Individual factors in healing

At the individual level, those who are predisposed by genetics to be more anxious than their peers are also more likely to develop PTSD symptoms in response to trauma, and thus increased vulnerability may be passed through generations (Xie *et al.* 2009). The enduring effects of sexual violence are also typically greater in individuals who have experienced or witnessed highly stressful events in childhood than in non-traumatised individuals. Indeed, neurobiological evidence shows that individuals with childhood sexual abuse-related PTSD typically display deficits in hippocampus, amygdala, medial prefrontal cortex and other limbic structures which are implicated in learning, memory, emotional regulation and resilience to subsequent life stressors (Anda *et al.* 2006).

However, individual characteristics can also contribute to individual resilience in the face and aftermath of traumatic events. For example, Valentine and Feinauer (1993) found that women survivors of childhood sexual abuse who had a more positive view of themselves tended to regain a sense of control more quickly and to draw effectively on social supports than those suffering from low self-esteem. Individuals who report reframing sexual assault as providing unexpected positive changes (for example, by promoting broadened perspectives, new coping skills, greater empathy or strengthened support networks) are less likely to develop post-traumatic symptoms (Frazier, Conlon and Glaser 2001). Moreover, the expression of positive emotion among young adult survivors of childhood sexual abuse predicts better adjustment and better social relations over time (Bonanno *et al.* 2007).

Finally, individuals' acquisition of appropriate coping skills in the aftermath of an experience of sexual violence can decrease the severity of its adverse effects long term. Learning about the neurobiological basis of trauma and engaging in self-care and self-soothing activities are some ways of coping that people may find helpful, but there is no rigid quick-fix. Often it will take time and practice to explore which strategies are helpful to each individual. Other strategies may be more destructive, in the sense of actually damaging the survivor in the long term. Alcohol or drug (legal or illegal) abuse, overeating or starving oneself and self-harm are all common examples of such strategies, but more generally any other type of behaviour that becomes compulsive (such as overworking, over-exercising, obsessive thrill-seeking, compulsive gambling or binge-shopping) can easily turn into an unhelpful strategy.

Social factors

While outlining differences in individual background and assault-specific factors, we are far from claiming that recovery from sexual violence occurs primarily within individuals or is determined by characteristics of the assault. Individuals are embedded within broader caregiving systems including their families, friends and communities, and survivors' responses to sexual trauma are intimately interconnected with the social environments they inhabit. We turn towards our trusted relationships to understand our fear and to receive comfort and soothe our stress response. This is particularly important in childhood, when coping strategies and self-soothing are established in relationships with caregivers. For example, when infants cry in pain or in fear, they are soothed by their caregivers through gestures such as rocking and holding, and through this type of interaction children learn to understand their internal states, and also how to control them (Siegel 2001). Indeed, a recent review of child responses to abuse shows that abused children who come from stable and supportive family environments have higher resilience than those without such support (Afifi and MacMillan 2011). Having trusting relationships can also help reaffirm feelings of self-worth – children who are able to learn coping strategies and have social support were found to be better adjusted as adults as measured by self-esteem and psychological symptomatology (Runtz and Schallow 1997).

As we grow into adulthood, support networks typically widen from the family network to include partners, friends and peers, as well as members of the wider community, including neighbours, religious leaders, health professionals and rape crisis workers. Characteristically, research on adult sexual assault survivors shows that higher levels of social support are associated with a variety of positive outcomes, including positive life change and growth, as well as reduced PTSD and depressive symptoms (Jacques-Tiura *et al.* 2010). Conversely, a lack of support by significant others can add to their distress and may collude with individuals' feelings of guilt and shame, precluding them from seeking out further help. Indeed, victims are too often blamed not only for the assault but also for coping poorly; see Ullman (1999) for a review of empirical studies of social support and sexual assault, in order to evaluate the evidence for the role of support in recovery from mental health and physical health consequences of this crime.

Trauma-informed care

Advances in our understanding of the complexities trauma and its effects on the whole person have allowed for the development of services designed to reduce psychological distress and restore a sense of wholeness and integration in survivors. These services can also help survivors to feel less alone, to normalise their experience, re-establish trust in themselves and others, and make connections between the mind and body. Within the therapy world, several approaches have shown some success, including cognitive processing therapy (Resick and Schnicke 1992), anxiety management, acceptance and commitment therapy, and eye movement desensitisation and reprocessing, to name but a few. Trauma-informed approaches are not the exclusive territory of therapists, but have also been adopted by other professionals such as law enforcement agencies, prosecutors, advocates and health agencies, with initiatives such as trauma-informed sexual assault investigation units, trauma-sensitive yoga and trauma education in group settings. Providing a review of all trauma-informed modalities and interventions is outside the scope of this book, and ultimately the type of service chosen may differ from one survivor to another, depending on the age, history and type of abuse, treatment setting, specific trauma symptoms and stage of healing.

Whatever the service, be this therapeutic or non-therapeutic (in as much as they are not specifically designed to treat symptoms or syndromes related to sexual violence), one key principle of best practice in our view is that the service should be informed about and sensitive to trauma-related issues present in survivors. Trauma influences how people approach and respond to services, making it essential that organisations serving survivors of sexual assault recognise expressions of trauma and acknowledge the role trauma plays in people's lives. Elliott and colleagues (2005) have developed ten governing principles to make services trauma informed. While these principles stem from a nine-site evaluation of primary substance abuse treatment, mental health and violence-against-women settings in the context of providing trauma-informed care for women, they can be adapted to provide trauma-informed care for survivors of sexual violence as well, and whatever their gender identity. Trauma-informed services need to:

1. recognise the impact of violence and victimisation on development and coping strategies
2. identify recovery from trauma as a primary goal
3. employ an empowerment model to help survivors regain power and agency over their lives
4. strive to maximise a survivor's choices and control over their recovery
5. be based in a relational collaboration
6. create an atmosphere that is respectful of survivors' need for safety, respect and acceptance
7. emphasise survivors' strengths, highlighting adaptations over symptoms and resilience over pathology
8. minimise the possibilities of retraumatisation
9. strive to be culturally competent and to understand each survivor in the context of their life experiences and cultural background
10. solicit clients input and involve clients in designing and evaluating services.

For our purposes of improving services for trans people, principle 9 could be explicitly expanded to include that all staff of an organisation must also understand each survivor in the context of their gender identity. Finally, we would add to the list that trauma-informed services must attend too to the needs of those who serve trauma survivors by providing the same elements of care to staff. Vicarious trauma – the cumulative effect of witnessing the suffering of others – is well documented in the caring professions, leading to negative changes to an individual's physical, psychological and spiritual health (Pearlman and Saakvitne 1995). Therefore, it is important to address the needs of organisations and staff in order to reduce and effectively respond to vicarious trauma.

Conclusion

In this chapter, we drew on neurobiological evidence to recognise the traumatic nature of sexual violence, and to emphasise how sexual violence can affect every level of a person's well-being, the way they feel about themselves, the way they feel about other people and the way they make sense of the world. What we have learned about the impact of sexual trauma can directly inform professionals' practice to support the healing and growth of survivors while avoiding retraumatisation. In presenting this information we were mindful of a number of points: survivors may experience none, some or many of the possible effects of sexual trauma at different times; there are likely to be impacts of sexual trauma that researchers have yet to identify; there is no single way a sexual violence survivor should look and act; trauma-related symptoms are not signs of illness, deficiencies or weakness, nor are they characteristics of the individual – rather, they are normal responses to trauma.

While we largely focused on the importance of a trauma-informed approach for the healing process of all survivors, a number of issues unique to trans survivors remain to be addressed to offer appropriate support. For trans survivors, their identities (and the discrimination they face surrounding those identities) often make them hesitant to seek help from police, hospitals, shelters or Rape Crisis Centres – the very resources that are supposed to help them. In the next chapter, we will explore further the barriers which trans survivors face when they consider accessing a service, as well as how organisations can begin to address those barriers.

Chapter 4
Problems with Accessing Mainstream Services

Introduction

Nearly every survivor of sexual violence faces barriers in accessing services at one time or another. But for trans survivors, barriers are often confronted far more frequently. Research shows that trans people face very high levels of discrimination, including while trying to access support services (Grant *et al.* 2011; James *et al.* 2016; McNeil *et al.* 2012). In our own research, we have found that trans survivors in particular face a variety of specific barriers in these situations (Rymer and Cartei 2015). Understanding how and why people access services to meet their perceived needs requires clarity about a number of factors that influence the behaviour of individuals, service professionals and the context they operate in at all points on the access route to services. Often these multiple barriers are experienced together, which can make it extremely difficult or even impossible for trans people to access services.

While some providers may be oblivious to these barriers, more often providers are keen to overcome these barriers but are unsure how to go about it. This chapter explores the barriers to accessing services for trans survivors of sexual violence, so that service providers can begin considering how to minimise them.

Exploring barriers: survivors' candidacy for sexual violence services

A concept that offers potential to understand access and utilisation is 'candidacy', which has been used to explain access to, and utilisation of, healthcare services (Dixon-Woods *et al.* 2006). According to the Candidacy Framework, an individual's successful access and use of services is jointly and dynamically negotiated between the individual and the service provider, and constrained or facilitated by factors at multiple levels – individual, socio-cultural, professional, organisational, structural and material. These factors are grouped into six dimensions:

1. **Identification** – the extent to which people recognise themselves as needing a service.
2. **Navigation** – awareness of the services on offer and the practicalities of accessing those services (including issues of accessibility).
3. **Permeability of services** – the ease with which people can use services. Services are more or less permeable depending on the ease with which users can access those services (for example, services requiring a referral are less permeable than drop-ins). This also includes the extent to which people feel comfortable with the organisational values of the service.
4. **Presentation** – the ability to self-present, communicate and articulate the 'need'. This relates also to the ability to voice concerns about the standard of service if those needs are not met.
5. **Professional adjudication** – the judgements and decisions made by professionals to decide whether the client is a

suitable 'candidate' for a service, that is, whether they can access and continue receiving the service.

6. **Operating conditions** – the perceived or actual resources available to provide a service for that client.

Using 'candidacy' to understand access to services by survivors of sexual violence

The Candidacy Framework can help us gain a more comprehensive understanding of the challenges trans and non-binary people face when accessing support. The following sections applies the framework to describe and understand the barriers commonly experienced by all survivors and by trans survivors in particular.

Identification

Many survivors may not feel that they can actually ask for support. Sexual violence is a highly stigmatised crime and, as a result, many survivors of rape and sexual abuse feel guilty and never talk about their experiences. Moreover, because the topic of sexual abuse is both personal and traumatising, many victims feel deeply ashamed. Media reports erroneously referring to rape as 'sex' can contribute to this shame, as can insensitive comments from loved ones, and rape myths and other elements of rape culture. This sense of shame causes some victims to go years without telling anyone of their abuse – a decision often later used against them as evidence that the assault or abuse never occurred, or that it was clearly not important enough for them to ask for help at the time. All of these cultural beliefs about rape create significant barriers in survivors of any gender in recognising and naming their experiences of sexual violence and sexual trauma.

Trans voices

'In the beginning, I believed that it was my fault. When time had passed I thought that support services would believe it had been too long and my memory might be wrong. I also thought that they might not think it was really rape because we were both DFAB (described as female at birth) trans, and because I was coerced into giving consent.'

'...Feeling that my experience wasn't that bad; not knowing what support was available; feeling that I wouldn't be believed; feeling like I was deviant for engaging in sexual behaviour and if I admitted it I would be shamed.'

Navigation

Awareness of what is available is crucial to accessing appropriate support. Some survivors become aware of specialist services while using community-based or statutory services. For example, a GP may provide a survivor with information about their local Rape Crisis Centre. Often, these community-based or specialist services are used as intermediaries and negotiate access to specialist services. They act as informal gateways to a wide variety of services, matching the needs presented by individuals with services that might meet them. Survivors may also find out about services in a variety of other ways, including through internet searches, word of mouth or information displayed in community spaces, for example on noticeboards.

Trans survivors face the additional barrier of being unsure how their gender identity will affect their ability to access sexual violence support services. Many struggle to identify support services which they are confident will be safe and helpful for them to use.

Trans survivors are often concerned that a support service may reject them because of their transgender identity or that they may experience discrimination within a service.

Trans voices

'We get so worried about potentially being turned away from support groups or having to spend a phone call explaining what a trans person even is, that we just don't access support.'

'I didn't know where was safe to access and who would take me seriously. I was also afraid that getting help could make things worse.'

Even if users are aware of services, they may not know how to access them, or they may find it difficult to access them because of the practicalities involved. For example, if a self-referral must be made prior to using a service, some service users may find it difficult to do so if they lack the practical resources (such as access to a computer or credit on their mobile phones) required to complete the self-referral process.

Other access practicalities include physical barriers that may prevent users from making use of the service they need. For example, a lack of lifts can prevent access by survivors with mobility problems, and a lack of outreach may mean that those living in more isolated areas may not be able to physically reach the location of an organisation or practitioner. Financial barriers, such as service fees, transport and childcare costs, can also prevent some survivors from gaining access to services.

Permeability of services

There are a wide range of recovery services for survivors of sexual violence, from voluntary sector organisations providing emotional support services to statutory services. At the time of writing this book, voluntary providers in the UK include: national organisations, such as Barnardo's, the Children's Society and the NSPCC (National Society for the Prevention of Cruelty to Children), delivering local services alongside a range of more local organisations; specialist women's support organisations, including the Rape Crisis Centres; and organisations supporting specific groups such as women and girls from black and minority ethnic (BME) communities. Statutory services include non-specialist services such as police, social services and the NHS.

These services have different levels of permeability according to both the accessibility pathways and survivors' circumstances. For example, free-at-the-point-of-access services are highly permeable for those who are financially disadvantaged, but, as Dixon-Woods *et al.* (2006) noted in relation to healthcare services, appointment systems may make those services less permeable to those without a fixed abode or who have a chaotic lifestyle, because they still require specific resources (such as stable addresses, being able to present in particular places at particular times). Given the higher levels of homelessness and mobility of trans individuals (James *et al.* 2016), these people are more likely to find it difficult to access services that require resources such as a fixed abode or reliable transport.

Survivors may have a wide range of needs, particularly in relation to mental health support, and these support needs may be exacerbated by the wider impact on their lives arising from the abuse they have experienced, including relationship problems and difficulties such as alcohol and substance misuse. The absence of a joined-up service response places the onus on survivors to access multiple services in the effort to address this multiplicity of needs. The recognition of the need for a more holistic approach to service provision has seen in recent years the emergence of 'one-stop-shop' services, whereby survivors typically access one centre comprising a multi-professional team (for example, psychologists, lawyers, medical professionals and other practitioners) often from different agencies, who offer medical, psychological and welfare support as required, and where survivors are capable co-creators of their own care plan and healing. One-stop-shop service models have, in recent years, been successfully developed globally in several settings for survivors of violence, including war-torn countries (Mukwege and Berg 2016).

The one-stop-shop approach, however, raises its own challenges. For example, clearly marked, stand-alone centres offering services exclusively to survivors are also likely to be known as such within communities and thus risk stigmatising people who are seen entering these premises. As one-stop-shops require multiple specialisms, they are usually delivered by agencies coming together, with all the challenges that partnership work brings, including co-ordination among providers, maintaining effective referral and information-sharing processes without breaking survivors' confidentiality, and agreeing common policies and procedures without threatening different agencies' ideological and financial independence.

Permeability is also dependent on the extent to which people feel aligned with the values of the service they are trying to access and their level of satisfaction on using the service. Therefore, survivors who distrust the one-stop shop may lose the opportunity to access not one but multiple services which are provided by it, thus raising further barriers. While there is no research on trans community perspectives on these models, studies on their effectiveness for other minorities such as BME individuals show mixed results. Specifically, individuals described distrust of one-stop-shop confidentiality, preferring services that catered for their own community or specialist services, while others preferred one-stop shops that were not confined to one community or issue (Griffiths, Gerressu and French 2008).

Survivors may already be extensive users of services, in particular health services, even without disclosure. In these cases, training professionals to identify sexual violence with a sensitive approach can be crucial to avoid 'blind spots'. In recognition of this, the concept of a 'no-wrong door' approach encourages frontline professionals as well as members of the public to think about their role in recognising sexual violence and to consider how to respond appropriately to disclosures. This model recognises that the first point of contact may not be the best equipped to meet the survivors' needs and thus promotes the offering of sufficient help with referrals and co-ordination so that help-seeking in itself is not inadvertently discouraged.

Presentation

The perception among survivors that the services on offer to them may or may not be 'for them' can stem from basic communication difficulties, such as language diversity in the services provided or lack of service provision for the visually and aurally impaired. It can also stem from too little sensitivity within services to equality and diversity issues in relation to sexual orientation, gender identity, disabilities, age, religious observance and cultural norms more generally. A further issue is that service users may feel that their knowledge is generally not valued or taken seriously by professionals, policy makers and services, and thus become cynical about the value and relevance of the service to them.

In recent years, there has been increasing emphasis placed on addressing these issues by involving users more closely in the planning, development and delivery of services. This is the result of a growing recognition that because of their direct experiences of using services, service users have a unique insight into what works, which can be used to improve services. In our own experience, we have found that trans survivors who access specialist services really value those services being run by trans people themselves.

Particularly for smaller organisations with limited resources, service user involvement can be hard to achieve. There are costs involved in recruiting service users in the first place, and setting up organisation-specific channels for them to get involved effectively may require a trial-and-error approach of involvement before finding the best model. Service user involvement also requires ongoing investment as service users can lose faith in the involvement process if they are not kept informed of what has or has not been done because of their involvement, or if there is no improvement to the service. Another issue is to ensure that the service users who are involved are representative of the wider user base, otherwise the risk is that they will be speaking from their own experience, however valuable, rather than offering their views as a 'representative sample'. Engaging a diverse range of service users includes investing in a diversity of methods for people to get involved and thinking about the commitment expectations placed on users. Finally, users need to feel they can express their views without impunity, as they may be worried about reprisals, especially if they are dependent on services.

Professional adjudication

Sexual violence is a morally loaded crime, linked to notions of culpability and victimisation. The victim's characteristics and their perceived 'behavioural responsibility' for avoiding social contexts commonly associated with the potential for violence can influence professionals in their views about which survivors are 'deserving' or 'undeserving' of their help. Assessments of 'deservedness' can also be made according to *who* the survivor is. For example, people with addictions and complex mental health needs may be denied access because of their perceived degree of unpredictability and dangerousness towards staff and other users. As a marginalised and stigmatised group within society, trans individuals are unlikely to be construed as 'innocent' victims. On the contrary, the idea of 'transsexualism' as dangerous – a threat both to individuals they have contact with and to national security and social order – has a long history.

Operating conditions

'Local' or 'context-specific' factors can influence decisions about subsequent service provision. Services often operate in different geographical localities under different financial landscapes, with differing degrees of tolerance towards trans individuals depending on the size of the trans community and their level of need. For example, according to the Trans Needs Assessment (Hill and Condon 2015), Brighton & Hove (in Sussex, UK) has a well-established local trans community (it is estimated that at least 2760 trans and non-binary adults live there) and, as it is seen as inclusive, many trans people who live elsewhere visit Brighton & Hove to socialise, study and work. Brighton & Hove is further characterised by the existence of a number of businesses, welfare and third-sector services and voluntary groups that maintain a focus on promoting trans awareness and inclusion. As a result, the majority of trans people in the city make use of the city's services, though trans people report that they still face abuse, discrimination and social isolation in the city.

Barriers to accessing service – trans survivors

Trans survivors experience additional barriers when they consider using support services. Some of these barriers are the same barriers described above, but they may be experienced more acutely by transgender survivors due to the other forms of discrimination and oppression which they already experience. There are additional barriers too that apply specifically to transgender survivors, which will be explained below.

Not knowing where to go

Many trans survivors worry that services will not be sufficiently skilled in working with transgender people. They are concerned that if staff and volunteers do not have a good understanding of transgender identities and the issues faced by trans people, the service user themselves will have to spend their time educating the service about these topics. As one survivor told us, 'I didn't have the resources to explain my gender on top of talking about my experiences of rape' (Rymer and Cartei 2015, p.158).

Survivors might also fear facing discrimination within a service. This fear of discrimination is well founded given the level of discrimination, violence and abuse experienced by the transgender community as described in Chapter 2. Quite often this discrimination and abuse is perpetrated by people who are generally expected to be safe, including family members and professionals who are meant to offer support and protection. For example, the *Injustice at Every Turn* report found that in the US, '22% of trans respondents who have interacted with police reported harassment by police, with much higher rates reported by people of color' (Grant *et al.* 2011, p.6). These experiences resulted in nearly half of respondents saying that they would be uncomfortable seeking police assistance. As one survivor told us, 'Previous bad experience with police and CPS (Crown Prosecution Service) meant I never reported this at the time and accessed services only when flashbacks became detrimental to my mental health' (survey respondent from original research, unpublished).

Another survivor told Forge, a US charity, about their experiences with violence while trying to access support services:

'I was homeless and desperately poor when the worst abuse took place. I was on welfare. The day I was beaten by 4 cops was at the welfare office. I reached out for help and I got bashed for it. Every time I tried to get help I was turned away. The welfare agency treated me as badly as the police did. What stopped me from getting the help I needed was the people I asked for help. Thankfully I found my own way within the system to get help. No thanks to the various agencies.' (munson and Cook-Daniels 2016, p.44)

These previous experiences of negative or harmful interactions with 'helping professionals' create a presumed lack of safety for trans people. It is reasonable in these circumstances to assume any new service or individual professional to be unsafe until they can prove otherwise. One survivor described this presumed lack of safety saying, 'I didn't know where was safe to access and who would take me seriously' (anonymous).

In order to remove these barriers and demonstrate the safety of your service, it is important to take proactive steps which will show transgender survivors that you are a safe place to turn for help. Such steps are outlined in detail in Chapters 5 and 6.

Fear of being outed

Many survivors are also very afraid of being outed (having their trans identity or history disclosed to others) by a support service. Outing can be intentional or unintentional but either way it can have terrible consequences for a survivor. Beyond simply being an experience that both is violating and creates a lack of trust, outing can also further expose trans people to discrimination or abuse. One survivor described their concerns saying, 'I was fearful that exposure in the national press would have resulted in my losing my job and everything that I had worked to achieve' (Rymer and Cartei 2015, p.158).

Lack of understanding about how gender identity and sexual violence may interrelate

Many transgender survivors worry that while accessing support services they will face misguided and harmful assumptions about how their experience(s) of sexual violence and their gender identity may relate to one another.

Some professionals or fellow service users may assume that a trans person was assaulted because of their gender identity and that the assault was consequently their own fault, as one survivor told us, 'People would tell me that I shouldn't have been "out" about being trans or that I shouldn't have transitioned because this would happen to me' (Rymer and Cartei 2015, p.158).

Others might face the assumption, particularly if their abuse was experienced during childhood, that their gender identity is a result of their experience with sexual violence – an assumption that is also sometimes made of gay, lesbian or bisexual people as well. A fear of these assumptions can cause transgender survivors to withhold information from medical professionals involved in their transition.

Trans voices

'[Not disclosing my experience with sexual abuse] was also because I didn't want it to jeopardise my chances of being allowed to transition by the GIC (gender identity clinic). I didn't want the GIC to think I was transitioning for the wrong reasons; I wanted them to think I was a perfectly average individual they would have no concerns about. In hindsight, I realise this was to my detriment, as what I experienced still causes me problems which might not be quite as severe had I sought support at the time.'

These cause-and-effect assumptions about survivors' experiences of violence and their gender identity ignore the highly individual ways in which identities are formed. If these assumptions are common within a service, it will create an environment in which transgender survivors do not feel safe enough to be honest and open about both their gender identity and their experiences of sexual violence. Such an environment is never conducive to a therapeutic healing process. Additionally, if one or more transgender survivors experience these emotions within a service, it is likely they will warn other potential service users away from the service in an effort to protect them from these harmful assumptions.

Talking about bodies

Services may also fail to take into account that asking survivors to discuss their bodies may cause additional distress for trans survivors who may already have a complex and at times painful relationship to parts of their bodies. This is particularly true in contexts where survivors may be asked to use (or hear others use) medicalised words to describe specific body parts. One survivor described how his concerns about how he would be asked to talk about his body stopped him from accessing services: 'As a trans man, I would have to use terminology for my genitals that is incredibly painful and dysphoria-inducing in order to explain what he did to me' (Rymer and Cartei 2015, p.158).

Trans voices

'It's hard to talk about experiences that relate to parts of my body which make me feel sick thinking about them, even without talking/thinking about abuse/rape. I feel as if talking about the abuse I have experienced invalidates my gender.'

If survivors experienced sexual abuse prior to their transition, this can create additional complexities in how they talk about the abuse, relate to the person they were at the time of the abuse, and discuss their bodies.

Trans voices

'Abuse/assault may have occurred when the trans person was perceived as a different gender by society, which makes things complicated. Psychologists sometimes want to tell us that we are trans because of the abuse faced. No one knows what language to use. Cis people don't get how to talk to trans people about sexual things even if they're not abuse related – never mind if they are. They don't get it.'

Finding the right words to use when discussing bodies and experiences can be very difficult. Finding ways to do this which are inclusive and helpful is discussed in detail in Chapter 6.

Lack of services for non-binary survivors

The fact that so many sexual violence recovery services are either 'for women' or 'for men' creates a significant barrier for non-binary individuals or any transgender individuals who, for whatever reason, do not feel comfortable or confident in accessing a 'women's service' or a 'men's service'. Some non-binary survivors do end up deciding to access services which are 'for women' or 'for men' but find that in order to maintain their access to these services they have to allow themselves to be consistently misgendered and they are not able to be open and honest about their gender identity. Many survivors shared with us the impact of this barrier.

> **Trans voices**
>
> '[I've been] unable to access any group services because I'm non-binary.'
>
> 'While I have considered contacting services for support, I've never done it because I'm not sure if I would be welcome as a genderqueer person, or whether providers would end up asking intrusive questions about my gender identity and linking it to my assault; and I don't want to undergo counselling or therapy or anything if I had to be misgendered throughout that process because I think I would find that more upsetting than helpful.'

'I'm neither a man nor a woman. All the services I could find were gendered. Even if I were binary, which at one point I thought I was (trans man), I'd be uncomfortable in such a place; as a trans man, being at a place for women would be completely wrong, but being at a place for male survivors would also be uncomfortable given I have a very hard time passing. Also, is feel the need to pretend to be cis, which would mean I would have to pretend most of the physical elements never happened.'

'I get read as a cis woman while identifying as a non-binary femme, and the services I used were "for women", which made me feel alienated and erased.' (Rymer and Cartei 2015, p.159)

'It was harder for me to access a service because of my gender identity. Many of the services were for women and because I didn't identify that way I couldn't access them, but I didn't feel safe in male spaces. I ended up accessing support from an LGBT charity/youth group.'

As expressed in the quotes here, many non-binary individuals find that they cannot comfortably use a 'women's service' or a 'men's service'. Given that the vast majority of sexual violence recovery services exist as single-gender services, this creates a tragic lack of services for most non-binary survivors. They find themselves unable to both be honest about their own gender and access valuable recovery services.

Sexual violence recovery services have a long history of operating as single-gender services and many such services understand this to be a vitally important part of their organisation. There is clear value in having single-gender spaces and many survivors find such spaces to be an important part of their healing. Yet, an unintended consequence of services running in this way is that non-binary survivors find themselves unable to access services. Some services have begun to recognise this unmet need and would like to expand their services in some way in order to increase access for non-binary survivors, but they have found that the funding streams which provide support to sexual violence recovery services restrict their ability to do this. The issue of how to adapt historically single-gender services (and the organisations that fund them) is a complex and in many instances controversial issue. But until the whole sexual violence recovery service sector grapples with this issue, non-binary survivors will continue to find themselves excluded from essential support. Chapter 7 will offer a more detailed discussion of this issue and potential ways forward for the sector.

Conclusion

All survivors face a difficult journey of accessing support following an experience, or a series of experiences, of sexual violence. Because of the cultural taboo around discussing sexual violence and the cultural tendency towards blaming victims of sexual violence for their own abuse, survivors of any gender often have to overcome feelings of shame and self-blame in order to seek out support. Survivors may also struggle to find the right services for them or, on discovering such services, they may find themselves unable to access these services due to practical barriers such as a lack of physical access or financial issues. Many potential service users also feel concerned about utilising services that do not present themselves as diverse and accessible organisations interested in and influenced by their users.

Transgender survivors face additional barriers on top of these existing barriers. Many trans survivors are understandably concerned that they will need to educate staff about transgender identities or that they may face discrimination within a service on the basis of their gender identity. They may also be concerned about being outed while using the service. Previous negative experiences with 'helping professionals' can create a presumed lack of safety for trans survivors, which makes it very difficult for them to feel safe enough to approach a service. Trans survivors may also worry that professionals working in support services could make hurtful and inaccurate assumptions about the relationship between their experience(s) of sexual violence and their gender identity. They may feel concerned too about how their bodies may be talked about or referred to while using a support service. Finally, non-binary survivors frequently find themselves entirely excluded from support services, which are very often single-gender services accessible to only men or only women. In order to offer truly accessible and safe services for trans survivors, all of these barriers must be considered and addressed. Doing just this will be the focus of the following chapters.

Chapter 5
Best Practice

Organisations

Introduction

Many professionals reading this book will work in organisations that have limited experience of supporting transgender individuals. Transgender survivors need many of the same things from your organisation as any other survivor using your services – a welcoming environment, to feel safe approaching you, and a physical space which meets their needs and keeps them safe. In order to offer this to transgender survivors, your organisation may need to make some changes to the way you work. This chapter will guide you through the various changes your organisation may need to make in order to offer transgender survivors a good-quality service.

Organisational ethos

Single-gender services
One of the first barriers organisations often face in working with trans survivors is the internal discussion among staff, volunteers and partner organisations about the organisation's own relationship to their service users' gender identities. The vast majority of

organisations in the sexual violence recovery sector began as 'women's services'. Many of these organisations were founded with (and continue to have) a strong feminist ethos. They recognise that women's voices, needs and concerns are far too often either ignored or suppressed in mainstream culture. These organisations also recognise that women are frequently subjected to gender-based violence, including sexual violence.

As a response to these concerns, women have been organising themselves, most notably in the Rape Crisis Movement, which has been in existence since the 1970s, to enable women to support and empower one another to heal from any form of sexual violence and abuse. Through these organisations, women also work together to bring about societal and cultural changes to the way in which all women are treated. The creation of women-only spaces offered, and continues to offer, an important opportunity for women to gather together in a way that feels safe. Healing, particularly healing from sexual violence, can rarely happen when one does not feel safe. As such, women-only organisations and spaces are key in establishing safety for women survivors.

This commitment to women-only services remains strong among many organisations in the sexual violence recovery sector, and women-only services are clearly valuable, providing much-needed safety and support to women who have survived sexual violence. As Rape Crisis England & Wales notes:

> The majority of generic and statutory services and spaces are gender neutral so it's important to us that we protect and maintain our safe women-only services and spaces for those who want and need them. Research conducted by the Women's Resource Centre (WRC) found that women who had used women-only services greatly valued this support, and an

independent poll of 1000 women across the UK found that 97% of those interviewed thought that a female rape victim should have the choice of accessing a women-only support service. (Rape Crisis England & Wales 2017a)

In more recent years, single-gender services have also been developed for male survivors of sexual violence. Services such as SurvivorsUK were established due to a recognition that male survivors of sexual violence often face significant stigma when disclosing their experiences of sexual violence and that there was a lack of services to support these men. These services also recognise a real value for male survivors in having male-only spaces where they can seek support.

Because of this history and the ongoing value of gender-based services, many organisations are hesitant to consider if or how they can support transgender survivors. Some worry that 'allowing' transgender women or men into their services will diminish the services that they already provide to cisgender individuals (Gottschalk 2009). The prospect of working with non-binary individuals raises further concerns for some organisations, a topic which is discussed in more depth in our final chapter.

While working through these concerns, organisations must bear in mind their obligations under the Equality Act 2010. A comprehensive guide on services' obligations to trans people under this legislation is available from the LGBT Domestic Abuse Project (2015) and Rape Crisis Scotland (2011). Under this legislation, transgender individuals are protected from discrimination, including the refusal of services. This means that in all but the most exceptional circumstances it is illegal for a single-gender service to refuse to offer a service to a trans person of that gender. The LGBT Domestic Abuse Project's guidance on this issue explains:

Where a trans woman is still in the process of transitioning, then there might be rare occasions requiring a service to be provided differently to her. Under the Equality Act 2010, people who provide separate and single-sex services, such as refuges, can only provide a service differently to a trans woman in a way which is less favourable compared to other women under exceptional circumstances. These circumstances depend on the facts of the individual case – this means that 'blanket' bans or policies barring people from accessing services are not acceptable. Discrimination against trans people is not acceptable and therefore the bar for a service provider to restrict service provision in this way is very high – the use of the exception has to be exceptional. Decisions made cannot be based on personal prejudice but on evidence of clear detriment to others, and even then the provider will need to show that a less discriminatory way to achieve the objective was not available. (2015, pp.14–15)

Organisations may have concerns about how they can meet these legal obligations while maintaining the value of their single-gender services, some of which will be discussed below.

One justification for excluding transgender people from certain spaces is that their presence would make cisgender people feel unsafe. As Evan Urquhart (2015) points out:

the justification for excluding trans women from certain spaces is that it is necessary in order to keep cisgender women safe from men. It's not always clear if the 'men' in these situations are supposed to be cisgender men cynically posing as trans women to gain access to women's only spaces or if it's an attempt to deny that trans women really are women; the line between the two tends to be blurred in anti-trans language.

This assumption also seems to imply that abuse cannot occur with people of our own gender, which is a myth as any same-gender abuse survivor can tell you. It also assumes that trans men (or trans women) are not 'real men' (or 'real women') because their physical sex organs may not match those of cisgender individuals. The false premise here is that biological sex and gender are the same thing. Even for cisgender individuals, there will be a diversity of biological sex characteristics from one person to another. For example, a cisgender woman may be born without her reproductive organs (as with sufferers of Mayer-Rokitansky-Küster-Hauser (MRKH) syndrome, for example) or have these removed later in life (for example, due to ovarian cancer), but this does not make her any less of a woman. Womanhood (or manhood) is not merely a function of one's biological makeup. Neither gender nor biological sex is quite as simple as what is on your birth certificate.

The other assumption often made by those attempting to exclude trans women from women's spaces is that trans women have experienced certain privileges while living within their assigned gender. For example, they may have been treated with more respect than those around them who were read as women, or they may have been able to safely walk alone at night in an area where this would not be safe for someone who was perceived as female. In our view, the 'male privilege' argument conflates the experiences of pre-transition trans women with those of cisgender men. Concerns about male privilege do not take into account that trans women have to deal with the inner reality of being a woman while being perceived as a man, and the likely discrimination resulting from this – particularly if unwilling or unable to adhere to strict notions of masculinity that being a 'man' in a patriarchal society entails.

Moreover, many trans women have felt their chosen gender their entire life. As the author Allison Gallagher (2017) writes, 'transgender women don't "live as men" before we transition – we live as women, coercively conditioned as men.' In addition, any male-related privilege is of course lost to transphobia and cisgender privilege post-transition, as the high rates of discrimination and transphobic violence presented earlier in the book testify.

Furthermore, in relation to trans women, once presenting as women, they are also subject to the misogyny that pervades our society and which other women experience, including increased threat of sexual violence. As Shon Faye (2017) comments in *The Guardian*:

> One line of attack I find particularly distressing is that we are trying to 'bully' our way into women's spaces such as refuges and rape crisis services. In their worst form, these arguments imply that I am trying to validate my gender identity by being recognised as a woman in these contexts. But the reason I want to be able to access women's spaces is because I now exist as a woman and I am treated as one in a misogynist society. Trans women are at least at the same risk as many other women from gendered violence. (21 November 2017)

Organisations should also consider the valuable contributions that transgender women can make to their women-only spaces. Transgender women are all too familiar with a daily struggle to survive and resist gender-based violence. In fact, the Human Rights Campaign found that, 'Transgender women face 4.3 times the risk of becoming homicide victims than the general population of all women' (2015, p.28). In the face of such heightened levels of violence, many transgender women have developed creative and enduring ways of coping. This strength and resilience is a valuable contribution to any women's group. As Professor Alison Phipps (2014) puts it:

How can we appreciate the social construction of the gender binary without listening to people who live in the spaces in-between? And conversely, how can we fathom how deeply felt the binary can be without the help of those who know they have been assigned to the wrong side?

It is encouraging to see many women-only organisations working proactively to end the view that trans men and women's rights are in some way in competition or opposition with the rights of cisgender men and women when it comes to accessing domestic and sexual violence services. In Scotland, a coalition of women's organisations released a joint statement saying, 'We do not regard trans equality and women's equality to be in competition or contradiction with each other... Rape Crisis and Women's Aid in Scotland provide trans-inclusive services on the basis of self-identification' (Engender 2017).

Gender-based services can maintain the positive aspects of offering a gender-based service while being accessible to trans individuals. These services must recognise that there is no single way to experience womanhood or manhood. As women and men of various different cultures, ages or life stages will bring a wide diversity of ways in which they experience and relate to their genders, so trans women and trans men will add to this diversity. They can bring their own unique gender experiences to the group, while maintaining the value and uniqueness of gender-based services.

Mixed-gender services

The fact that mixed-gender recovery services are open to people of any gender does not automatically make them safe for transgender survivors. Many mixed-gender services articulate their work and operate in a cisgender binary fashion, and thus fail to take into account the specific needs of trans people and non-binary survivors. They may not consider that some of those accessing their services are not cisgender and that transgender individuals can still face transphobia from users and staff in mixed-gendered spaces. For these services, it is also vital that they take considered steps in order to ensure their services are safe and accessible for transgender survivors. This will include recognising that non-binary people may access their services. In order to better recognise and include non-binary survivors, it is preferable to consider mixed-gender services as 'all-gender services' rather than 'gender-neutral services'. This helps to avoid the assumption that mixed-gender services are only for men and women. It also enables services to consider the role that their clients' gender identities play in their lives rather than making the assumption that gender never needs to be considered since the organisation works with people regardless of their gender. A full discussion of this topic as well as other ways to better serve non-binary survivors can be found in the final chapter.

For any organisation wishing to increase their accessibility for trans and non-binary people, delivering a high-quality service for them may call for new skills and knowledge. The rest of this chapter will focus on how organisations can change to become more accessible to and welcoming of transgender clients.

Training staff

In organisations that are determined to be open and accessible to transgender survivors, staff and volunteers may initially feel ill-equipped to confidently support these survivors. This is in itself a major barrier to creating a safe and welcoming environment for transgender people. The feeling of being 'unskilled' in meeting the needs of a particular population can be expressed in a variety of ways, including appearing nervous and anxious or seeking to avoid situations that elicit these feelings. For a trans survivor approaching such anxious or uncomfortable workers for support, these understandable feelings may come across to the survivor as 'my presence makes you uncomfortable'. If this message is conveyed to a potential client, it is unlikely that they will feel safe accessing your services.

Fortunately, organisations can do many things to equip their workers and volunteers to meet transgender survivors with an attitude of understanding and compassion. As a basic step, all workers and volunteers should learn about transgender identities and issues. This could be part of an organisation's ongoing equality and diversity training and a mandatory part of any worker and volunteer's induction. Any basic trans awareness training should cover information about transgender identities, including:

- the differences between sex and gender
- the diversity of non-binary gender identities
- the language and terminology used to describe various gender identities
- the importance of using the correct pronouns
- questions that should not be asked about a person's gender identity, their body or their gender experiences
- basic information about the transition process, including the the diversity of ways this is approached and experienced by transgender people
- discrimination and oppression faced by transgender people.

Once staff are equipped with this basic knowledge about trans people, they will be able to feel more confident in working with transgender clients. This confidence will support staff in making clients feel comfortable while accessing services. This basic training will also help staff to avoid using language or asking questions which may make transgender clients feel uncomfortable, unsafe or hurt.

If sourcing this type of training is a concern for your organisation, it may be worth considering a training swap with a local LGBT charity or organisation. Many LGBT charities would be eager to offer their staff and volunteers basic training about sexual violence, and happy to offer trans awareness training in exchange. If your organisation is a member of Rape Crisis England & Wales and has access to its Workforce Development Programme, a module on working with transgender survivors is available within this programme. It is strongly recommended that trans people are involved in providing any trans awareness training to your workers, either as sole or co-facilitators of the training. While no one trans person can represent the needs and experiences of all trans people, nevertheless they will have lived knowledge of at least some of the issues discussed, and by this person providing the training, trainees will have an opportunity to meet an out trans person, perhaps for the first time. Having met and spent time with a trans person will likely help decrease any anxiety in workers and this in turn will help trans service users to feel more welcome.

It is essential that such training is revisited often, both as standalone training and in terms of how it is integrated into the ethos of your organisation. This should be done in the same way that organisations work to regularly revisit and improve the way they work with other marginalised groups. As one participant in our research put it:

'...ensuring ALL employed from a front desk to senior levels are educated in human rights and that an "equal opportunities" policy does not simply "exist" to gloss the image of that organisation but is a constant reminder that should you meet people with a protected characteristic they must be treated with respect and dignity.' (Rymer and Cartei 2015, p.159)

Communication, interaction and physical spaces

Once staff have a basic awareness of transgender identities and issues, it is important to think about all the ways in which your organisation communicates with the public in order to make these communications trans inclusive.

This work is essential because many transgender survivors will understandably assume that organisations will not be safe places for them unless the organisation proactively demonstrates otherwise. This mistrust towards other services is typically due to past experiences of exclusion, harassment or discrimination within other organisations. In our research a professional commented: 'People are not coming forward because they have a very strong learnt experience of being excluded' (Rymer and Cartei 2015, p.159).

Due to these previous experiences, it is essential that organisations take proactive steps which will demonstrate to transgender survivors that they will be safe while using your services. Further guidance on this issue can be found in the Stonewall publication, *Getting it Right with Your Trans Service Users and Customers* (2016).

Promotional materials and resources

Organisations should resolve to use more inclusive and welcoming language in describing themselves and the diversity of survivors they serve.

If your organisation serves women/men only, does it currently describe itself as 'for women'/'for men', or 'for female'/'for male' survivors? This language can immediately create a feeling of rejection in trans women and trans men, as it is unclear if they would be welcomed into your service. If you are a service that works only with women or only with men, it is better to describe your organisation as one that works with 'self-identifying' women or men. This term makes it clear that your organisation will welcome any people whose own gender identity is that of a woman or a man, including trans women and trans men. It gives the important message that you understand gender to be a matter of self-identification rather than a biologically determined aspect of someone's identity. Avoid the use of the words 'female' or 'male' as these are often understood to describe sex rather than gender.

If your organisation, or specific services within it, works with anyone regardless of their gender, it is better to describe these services as being for people of 'any gender' rather than 'for men and women'. The latter alienates those who would not describe themselves as fitting neatly in either category, such as non-binary individuals. Eighty-three per cent of participants in our research (Rymer and Cartei 2015) said that they would feel uncomfortable accessing a service that advertises itself as 'for women' or 'for men' (p.159). Not only does such language create barriers for transgender survivors considering using your service; it can also create assumptions among staff and other survivors in group environments about the gender identity of those using your service. As one survivor who was using a 'for women service' told us: 'I get read as a cis woman while identifying as a non-binary femme, and services I used were "for women", which made me feel alienated and erased' (Rymer and Cartei 2015). Healing is unlikely to happen in an environment that makes a survivor feel alienated and erased.

Ensuring that the gender-related language you use to describe your organisation and services is trans inclusive is key to removing many of the initial barriers which stop transgender survivors from stepping through your doors in the first place.

You can also consider including the following in your publicly available material:

- adding links on your website and social media pages to trans organisations
- making posters and marketing materials for trans organisations available for staff and service users, for example in leaflet stands in your building or on stalls you host at events
- developing a printed or online resource targeted at trans people who may need your services.

Regardless of whether you are a single-gender or a mixed-gender service, your organisation should have a clear and publicly available Transgender Policy, which describes in clear terms what your organisation has done and is committed to doing on an ongoing basis in order to ensure that trans people are able to safely use your services. This policy should cover who can access your services; what training staff and volunteers receive about transgender identities; what you have done to ensure your forms and physical environment are accessible for transgender clients; what your organisation will do if a transgender person faces discrimination or harassment while using your services; and your policies on supporting transgender employees.

Monitoring and evaluation

Your organisation should also develop a framework which supports safe, confidential and appropriate monitoring of the needs of trans people accessing your organisation. This can be done by framing monitoring and evaluation as a participatory process in which service users, who are the primary stakeholders, are involved as active participants at its various levels. Participatory monitoring and evaluation (M&E) has increasingly received attention, and here we will not attempt to replace any of the many good books written on the subject (such as Valadez and Bamberger 1994; Gosling and Edwards 2003; Chambers 1997; Estrella *et al.* 2000; Parks *et al.* 2005). We would, however, like to highlight a few important points.

First, in order to ensure that there is consistent and meaningful engagement and involvement by users in M&E, it is helpful to develop an M&E plan to map out what information is needed from service users and how it will be used. With shared understanding of the overall purpose, the next step is to clarify the scope of the M&E process. 'Scope' relates to the extent and degree of sophistication of the M&E systems that will be used. This in turn will depend on the organisational resources available to dedicate to M&E and what sort of information will be needed. The plan will also include the service users' journey through the organisation and the point(s) in that journey where service users' information and feedback will be actively sought. This may include, to name a few, verbal feedback from service users at mid-point and after receiving a service, evaluation surveys and interviews, and regular user forums.

In addition to hosting regular user forums, organisations may wish to set up their own trans network groups outside the organisation or tap into existing ones. Trans network groups offer a formal mechanism for trans people, both service users and non-service users, to come together to share information and support on issues they experience in accessing services. For example, as part of the Trans Needs Assessment (Browne *et al.* 2015), Brighton & Hove City Council hosted a series of focus groups, alongside other activities. These meetings allowed trans people to contribute their experiences, knowledge and skills to help address problems that trans people in the city were facing. Networks of this kind give marginalised groups an opportunity to be heard. Such networks may also encourage trans people to access the services that participate in these processes and encourage organisations to educate non-trans staff on how to support and understand trans colleagues and service users. These broad networks of trans people also allow specialist organisations, like sexual violence recovery services, to hear from individuals who normally would not come in contact with their organisations. The ideas and experiences of these individuals can be invaluable in raising issues that the organisation had not previously considered.

Involving clients in M&E should also be balanced with minimising the burden for M&E on the service users themselves, i.e. not overwhelming them with feedback requests, collecting information at unsuitable points, or gathering data that will actually not be used.

On the specific point of monitoring gender identity, consideration ought to be given to the forms you ask new service users to complete, including intake forms and equality forms. For example, it is best to use a blank field for gender so that service users are able to define their own gender in the way which feels most honest, rather than being restricted to a pre-selected list of options. If your organisation determines that a list must be given, ensure that the options listed include a wide variety of gender identities (including non-binary identities) rather than a simple 'male', 'female' and 'other'. Suggesting that transgender individuals are 'other' is very far from welcoming and inclusive. It is also worthwhile to ask new clients to identify their pronouns on intake forms, so long as there is a mechanism in place to ensure these pronouns are then constantly used by staff. Ensuring that your forms reflect a diversity of gender identities is an important part of ensuring that transgender individuals are treated with respect and validation within your organisation.

Finally, participatory M&E also means that the flow of communication is not just a one-way system in which information from clients is used by the organisation to evaluate its services against track indicators for internal use and/or to report back to funders and commissioners. Clients need to know how the information they provide will be used, and what changes will or have been made in response to it and why.

Making your building a safe place for transgender survivors

It is important that the physical space of your organisation is safe for those transgender survivors who do come through your doors. One of the most 'talked about' aspects of creating physical safety for transgender people is ensuring that they have safe toilets to use. Trans people often have experiences of being unsafe while using toilets.

> **Trans voices**
> 'Being refused from toilets is heartbreaking. It happens more often than I want to think about, and on more than one occasion I have been threatened with violence if I stayed in the male toilets.'

If there are single-stall toilets in your building, there is no reason why these need to be labelled for a particular gender. A sign reading 'toilet' or 'WC' will do just fine. Alternatively, there are 'gender-neutral toilet' signs available to purchase or to print. It is important that at least one such single-stall toilet is available as a gender-neutral toilet so that anyone who feels unsafe using a toilet with other people present has an available and safe toilet. Where this toilet is also the disabled-accessible toilet, it may be useful to label it in a way which denotes that it is both an accessible and gender-neutral toilet. If no single-stall toilets are available in your building, consideration should be given to making the multi-stall toilets gender neutral. If you have two or more sets of multi-stall toilets and are concerned that some women who use your service would not feel safe using a gender-neutral multi-stall toilet, you could consider making one set of multi-stall toilets gender neutral while the other is for women only.

It is equally important that transgender people's right to use a multi-stall toilet which corresponds to their gender identity is protected. As one of the survivors we interviewed said, 'If I go to the toilets and get challenged and report it...the organisation shouldn't say to me "you better use the accessible toilets"' (Rymer and Cartei 2015, p.159).

To ensure that survivors are given all the options for which toilet to use, any service user should be told where each of the toilets are located when they ask for directions, regardless of their presumed gender identity.

Challenging transphobia

It is also important that your staff and volunteers are equipped to challenge any harassment or discrimination a service user could face while accessing your service. This may be directed at the service user by other service users, other individuals in your building (if it is a shared building), or staff and volunteers from your organisation. As a service provider, you have a responsibility to ensure that your organisation works in a sensitive and respectful way with anyone who has a protected characteristic as defined in the Equality Act 2010. Transgender individuals are included as a group of people who have a protected characteristic under this legislation. This legislation requires that transgender people using your services be protected from direct and indirect discrimination. Such discrimination should be dealt with in the same way as any other form of discrimination or harassment (such as racial, misogynistic and ableist). It should be swiftly addressed and a clear message should be given to both parties that such behaviour is not acceptable within your organisation where everyone has a right to be safe. The person being harassed should receive support after the incident and a conversation should be had about any support they may need in order to manage the fear or anxiety which the incident may provoke if they use your service again. The person who harassed the transgender individual should also be spoken to in order to help them understand the impact of their behaviour and to set expectations around what is expected of them (and all service users) when accessing your services.

Similarly, it is important that as an organisation you are active in challenging transphobia in the public arena. There are still individuals and groups that refuse to accept that transgender women are 'real women' and claim that their presence in women-only spaces is an 'intrusion' (for example, '"Reclaim The March!" Statement from Radical Feminists on what occurred at London Reclaim the Night' (GenderTrender 2014)). As an organisation, you can make a public stand not to condone anti-transgender rhetoric whenever you are engaged in dialogue with such groups. You can also choose to avoid supporting events that fail to acknowledge the identities and experiences of trans women, and, when appropriate, public statements can be issued explaining why this is. Doing so also sends a powerful message to transgender survivors that they are valued and welcomed by your organisation.

Building links with trans organisations

In demonstrating to potential clients that you are a safe organisation for transgender survivors, it is also important to develop relationships within the trans community and specifically with local transgender activists and community leaders. Doing so will develop your organisation's understanding of the needs of the local transgender community and it will also allow you to develop trust with the community. Generally speaking, the transgender community is well networked and often individuals will rely on each other for recommendations about what organisations are safe and welcoming and which are not.

This community-building work is slow but valuable. As one professional told us:

> 'You have to take a long-term, slow trust building approach. It has to become an integral part of what you do, not a 6-month project. A lot of trans people have a really good bullshit radar. They know when an organisation is being tokenistic, and when genuine.' (Rymer and Cartei 2015, p.159)

What would this community-building work look like? It may involve larger projects like working on joint projects and campaigns with LGBT or trans organisations (such as tackling street harassment or hate crime together). In a recent blog post supporting the Equal

Recognition Campaign and reform of the Gender Recognition Act, Close the Gap, Rape Crisis Scotland and Scottish Women's Aid stated:

> For over a decade, we have engaged in constructive dialogue with our colleagues in the Scottish Trans Alliance, Equality Network, LGBT Youth Scotland and Stonewall Scotland. We have shared knowledge, explored complex practicalities and developed sensible policy positions on trans inclusion. We do not regard trans equality and women's equality to contradict or be in competition with each other. We listen carefully to each other's ideas and concerns and collaboratively create solutions, including the maintenance of women-only spaces and services. Rape Crisis and Women's Aid in Scotland provide trans inclusive services on the basis of self-identification. (Close the Gap 2017)

Other activities may include one-off commitments like having stalls at various Pride events, or things as simple as ensuring you have information available about trans services more generally in your venues and vice versa. Participants in our research were clear that these connections would go a long way in them trusting an organisation. In our survey, 70 per cent of respondents said they would feel comfortable using services in an organisation which worked with the LGBT community even if that organisation itself was not a specialist LGBT organisation (Rymer and Cartei 2015, p.160). Becoming a visible and trusted presence within your local trans community will be an essential part of how you demonstrate to potential clients that they will be safe and welcomed when they use your services.

If you are considering hosting a specialist service for trans survivors, it may be wise to enter into a formal partnership with an LGBT or trans charity and jointly deliver this service. For example, the authors of this book have been involved in setting up a helpline for trans survivors of sexual violence. This helpline has been run as a joint project between a local Rape Crisis Centre and a local LGBT charity. Together, these two organisations are able to provide the expertise necessary to run this project far better than either organisation would be able to do individually.

Trans voices: how to make services better

'Be explicit in saying whether or not services are open to trans people, and whether any trans inclusive services are open only to trans women, or if they are also open to trans men and non-binary people. Be explicit in whether or not trans inclusive services are provided by trans staff members. If services are intended to be trans inclusive, the user-base should not be gendered across material used by the service (for example, Rape Crisis England & Wales refers a lot to "women and girls" on its website and in its literature – a trans inclusive service should not use this gendered language).'

'Train staff in trans awareness and specifically state that the service is trans friendly.'

'Have trans exclusive support services or LGBT inclusive support services which are easy to access and widely available.'

'Asking pronouns and not assuming gender identity or sexuality would be a good start.'

'Have trans people working at the support service. Make sure people know the different bodies people of different genders can have – not just assuming the crotches and body configurations of people. Degender language around abuse and rape. Have specific, explicit policy for trans people.'

Auditing your accessibility tool

To gain a clear idea of what your organisation needs to change in order to become accessible to and welcoming of transgender clients, consider undertaking an audit of your publicity, forms, policies, training, physical environment and so on. The following chart includes a series of questions as well as suggested actions to address the necessary changes across various areas of your organisation.

Table 5.1: Accessibility and safety audit

Item to check	Suggested action
Have your staff had training on working with transgender individuals?	Information about transgender identities and experiences should be part of your organisation's equality and diversity training. Ideally, stand-alone courses will also be offered in order to achieve a greater depth of learning. If sourcing this training is a problem for your organisation, consider organising a training swap with a local LBGT organisation.

What gender-related language is used in your advertising (website, Twitter, Facebook, flyers and so on)?	It is better to use 'self-identifying women' rather than 'females'. If you work with people regardless of gender, use 'all genders' instead of 'men and women' (which excludes non-binary individuals).
Do the images on your website and in your publicity material include sufficient gender diversity?	Consider updating your images to include a larger diversity of gender expressions. You may also consider having a transgender flag in the footer of your website after you have made necessary changes to ensure your organisation is safe and accessible for transgender service users.
If different services offered by your organisations are offered to different groups of people, is this clear on your website? For example, if your advocacy service is for all genders but your helpline is for only self-identifying women, are you clear about this?	Be sure there is a clear and concise guide to gender-related service criteria on your website. If you do offer some services to people of all genders but overall advertise yourself as a 'women's organisation', consider the impact of this on service users of other genders accessing your 'all-gender' services.
Do your intake forms allow for a variety of gender expressions?	Change the 'gender' field on your forms to a free response rather than a multiple-choice response.

Item to check	Suggested action
Does your organisation have links with the trans organisations in your area?	If you do not, work on developing these relationships. Find ways you can work together and support one another.
Do you have an easily accessible Transgender Policy on your website?	If you do not have one, develop one.
Do you have at least one gender-neutral toilet available?	If you currently only have 'male' and 'female' toilets, designate at least one toilet as a gender-neutral facility.
Are your staff and volunteers clear on how to challenge discrimination and harassment if they witness it?	If not, revise your training to include these skills.

Conclusion

By making these fairly straightforward changes your organisation will come a long way in creating a safe and welcoming environment for trans service users. This type of environment is absolutely essential if any healing is going to happen. In the next chapter, we look in detail at what individual practitioners can do when working with transgender survivors to ensure they receive the best care and support possible.

Chapter 6
Best Practice

Individual Practitioners

Introduction

This chapter will focus on how individual practitioners in a variety of settings can best support trans survivors of sexual violence. A wide variety of professionals may need to support transgender survivors, including therapists, advocates, helpline workers, doctors and nurses, police officers and solicitors.

In this chapter, you will find advice on what kind of support trans survivors might need, how these needs may differ from those of other survivors, and how you can best meet those needs including how you can help survivors navigate other services they may wish to access.

At the end of the chapter, you will find key advice for a variety of professionals, including therapeutic professionals, independent sexual violence advocates, medical staff, and police and legal professionals.

What kind of support might transgender survivors require?

Like any survivor of sexual violence, trans survivors often require support from a variety of professionals as they attempt to recover from their traumatic experiences.

Some survivors require immediate medical assistance to address issues such as sexually transmitted diseases and pregnancy testing and treatment, or treatment of injuries sustained during an assault. These services are commonly offered by accident and emergency departments and GP surgeries, as well as sexual assault referral centres. The latter also provide specialist support to collect forensic evidence.

Survivors may make the decision to report to the police and will require support from specialist police officers as well as solicitors should their case be taken to court. Many specialist support agencies offer an independent sexual violence advocate whose main role is to provide specialist practical support to survivors who are considering reporting their experience to the police or are taking part in a criminal investigation.

Many survivors choose to access individual or group therapy, support helplines or online forums. Staff and volunteers who provide any of these forms of support may at times need to offer support to a transgender survivor, even if they work in mainstream services.

This chapter will provide guidance that all such workers should find helpful in providing this support. We acknowledge, however, that many more professionals may be involved, directly or indirectly, in supporting transgender survivors, and it is our hope that many of the principles outlined in this chapter will be of relevance to other supportive roles.

Supporting a survivor of sexual violence can be daunting; many people are afraid of saying or doing 'the wrong thing', or of 'damaging' someone further because they 'don't know enough'. While expertise is required for specialist and ongoing assistance, you don't need to be an expert to provide some level of support. If you bear in mind and put into practice some basic principles about what survivors find helpful, survivors will be able to guide you in what they need to heal.

The following basic principles for supporting survivors utilise the rich knowledge and experience of those working in the sexual violence sector, and particularly the Rape Crisis England & Wales National Service Standards (2012) and its training programme for professionals working in the sexual violence sector (2017b), as well as our own research and experience.

Within each section, you will also find practice examples specific to the various principles. It is hoped this will provide an opportunity to clarify how theory can be put into practice.

After discussing these basic principles, which apply to survivors of any gender, we will move on to describe best practice principles for supporting transgender survivors specifically.

Basic principles for supporting survivors

Listen

First and foremost, supporters must create the time and space to hear a survivor's story in as much (or as little) detail as the survivor needs to tell it. This listening should be empathetic, non-judgemental and offer an appropriate but non-shocked reaction to the pain caused by the survivor's experiences. Listening in this way enables survivors to know it is safe to tell their story and that their experiences will not cause you to turn away from them.

Survivor: I don't really know where to start.

Supporter: You can start wherever you feel comfortable starting, and share as much or as little as feels right to you. If you'd like to tell me about what happened, that's fine or we can just talk about how it is affecting you now if you would rather.

Survivor: It was really awful and happened for a long time, most of my childhood. Really terrible stuff, I am sure you don't want to know all about it.

Supporter: I am here to listen to anything that would be helpful for you to share. Some survivors find it helpful to explain exactly what happened, whereas for others going over all that again is not helpful. But I am here to hear whatever you need to share, no matter how awful.

Survivor: Okay, well it started when I was 5...

Believe and validate

It is essential that supporters make it clear to survivors that they are believed and that the abuse was not their fault. These two messages are key in the healing process. No matter how or when it happened, or your ideas about how a survivor should or shouldn't act, recognise the impact that sexual violence has had on the survivor. Recognise their courage for choosing to disclose to you. All survivors, regardless of gender, benefit from this type of empathetic and empowering support.

Survivor: I knew him and I let him into my room that night. And we'd been drinking a lot. Maybe I was not protecting myself well enough. Maybe in some way it was my fault?

Supporter: It's not your fault. No matter how much either of you had to drink or anything you did earlier in the evening, it was his responsibility to stop when you said no. And he didn't.

Survivor: I just feel like I can't call it rape or tell any of my friends about it. They saw me walk off with him that night; what if they think I just regret it now or that I should have known better? But at the same time, if it wasn't rape, how could it be making me feel so depressed and so afraid?

Supporter: It takes a lot of courage to call it rape when there are all these voices making you feel shame and guilt about what happened. By coming here today and naming it as what it is, you're being courageous and taking the first steps towards healing.

Let the survivor be in control

Sexual violence is an abuse of power, both in terms of the perpetrator overlooking the survivor's wishes in order to satisfy their own, and in terms of the way society supports a patriarchal system that views others as property, while also rewarding those who exercise power and control over others with no regard for human rights or dignity. Our work with clients recognises the fundamental importance of not reflecting these dynamics if clients are to be safe and healing is to occur. This means acknowledging and articulating the power dynamic inherent in a supportive relationship, as well as redressing a sense of powerlessness by responding to survivors as people with dignity and rights. It also means resisting the urge to 'take over' or to 'save', and instead recognising that survivors are the experts of their own healing. As such, our role is to help them recognise their own strengths and build on these, to explore options together so that they can make informed choices, and to respect these choices.

Survivor: I have been so depressed lately. I know there are probably things I could be doing to try to make that better, but I feel like I don't know where to start.

Supporter: What sorts of things do you think might help?

Survivor: Well, people keep telling me to go to my GP but I really don't want to take medication. It just doesn't seem right to me and I'm worried about the side effects, too.

Supporter: That's okay. Medication helps some people, but it's just one tool in the toolbox. It isn't for everyone. What else have you been thinking might help?

Survivor: Well, I think it would help if I was seeing other people more often.

Supporter: A lot of people find that it does help their depression to spend more time with other people. Is that something that has helped you before when you were depressed?

Survivor: Yeah, last time I was really depressed it really helped me when I started going to the art group. I think it was good for me to get out and spend time with other people who also got it and didn't make me feel anxious or weird.

Supporter: That's great. Is that art group something you could start going to again?

Survivor: Well, that group has ended now.

Supporter: That's a shame. I have some information about other similar groups that are running now. Would you like to see that information?

Survivor: Yeah, that would be good.

Best practice principles for supporting transgender survivors

Trans survivors may require additional knowledge and skills from their supporters above and beyond the skills and attitudes outlined above. These elements of best practice that are particularly relevant when supporting trans survivors will be the subject of the remainder of this chapter.

Establishing trust

As mentioned in previous chapters, many trans individuals have endured negative, oppressive or even violent experiences with service providers in the past. This history will mean that many trans survivors will assume services to be unsafe until proven otherwise. This is a reasonable assumption if the majority of previous interactions with services were painful or damaging. Indeed, it is an assumption made out of a need to protect themselves from further pain. Thus, it is the responsibility of service providers to demonstrate that their services are indeed safe for trans survivors and to build trust with both these individuals and the transgender community more widely.

The previous chapter examined what organisations can do to build trust between themselves and the transgender community. This section will examine how practitioners can form trusting relationships with individual transgender survivors.

As soon as possible after meeting a trans survivor, several messages should be conveyed to them in order to establish trust. First, it should be made clear that you respect their gender identity and that you will use whatever name, pronouns and other gender-related language they prefer. It is also worth speaking early on about whether they would like you to correct other people (for example, other professionals) should they misgender the survivor. The extent to which you can discuss their gender identity with others should be clarified early on too, as concerns around confidentiality may cause significant stress and worry for transgender individuals.

For both you and the survivor with whom you are working, these initial conversations can be tricky and anxiety inducing. To help facilitate trust-building and to gather all the information they need you to know about their gender identity, it may be helpful to offer a survivor the opportunity to provide you with this information in writing rather than verbally, either before you meet them or during your initial meeting. The 'How best to support me' forms found in the Appendix provide a template that could be used for this purpose.

It may also be useful to discuss early on what the survivor would like you to do to support them if they were to face discrimination or oppression within your organisation or if they felt their needs were not being met by your service. Many survivors will understand that your organisation may be in the initial stages of learning how to support trans survivors. By recognising this together and committing to working with them through any potential difficulties, you are likely to build trust that will endure through any problems you may face together.

The formation of a trusting relationship with trans survivors can be greatly aided by having a frank conversation about their gender identity and what they need from you in order to feel that their identity is respected and valued within your organisation. Survivors should also know that you will work to ensure they are safeguarded from discrimination and oppression within your organisation and that you will respond appropriately if they do face discrimination, oppression or inadequate service provision.

Connecting gender identity and experiences of sexual violence

Trans survivors have been clear in our research that one very important aspect in the support they receive is the internal views held by staff about the connection (or lack thereof) between the survivor's gender identity and their experience(s) of sexual violence. For example, some professionals believe that trans survivors are transgender as a result of the trauma they have experienced (particularly if this trauma occurred in childhood). Others believe that transgender survivors were assaulted as a result of being transgender and because of this the transgender survivor was in some way 'at fault'.

One survivor told us, 'People would tell me that I shouldn't have been "out" about being trans or that I shouldn't have transitioned because this would happen to me' (Rymer and Cartei 2015, p.158). Another survivor told Forge:

> 'I'm afraid to go anywhere for help, because they will say my transgenderism is related to abuse, or that I somehow egged it on by being a freak. I do not want to have it affect my ability to rightfully claim my own identity. I was transgendered before I was ever abused, but I don't think they will understand.' (munson and Cook-Daniels 2016, p.39)

It is absolutely key for professionals to understand that a survivor may not feel there is any cause-and-effect link between their gender identity and their experience of sexual violence. The fear that this will be a professional's view stops many transgender survivors from accessing services. Given this, the intention that you will be led by each survivor's own understanding of their gender identity and their experiences of sexual violence should be made clear to survivors as early as possible, including in publicly available information about your service (for example, on your website).

Similarly, practitioners must be led by survivors' own experiences and understanding when attributing difficult emotions to either a survivor's experience of sexual violence or to their gender identity. As one survivor told Forge:

> '[Providers could use] *lots* more education and understanding about transgender issues, the variety of experience, and the unique way it may impact the way we feel or cope as survivors (understanding the difference between feelings that are a result of sexual abuse and feelings that are a result of being trans; not trying to reduce everything to sexual abuse in order to wash over or ignore trans issues).' (munson and Cook-Daniels 2015, p.82)

Transgender survivors often have a complex understanding of the way their experience of sexual violence and gender identity (as well as any emotional pain which may be connected to each) interact. These understandings are varied and unique to each individual. Practitioners should believe neither that the two are always related in any particular way nor that they are never related; instead, they should be led by the survivor's own understanding of these complex dynamics.

Talking about bodies

Practitioners must also be aware that discussing, examining or touching trans survivors' bodies should be approached with extra care. Many transgender individuals experience significant dysphoria related to their body, often around parts of their bodies which may not fully match their gender identity (such as genitals, breasts, facial or body hair, and curvy or particularly flat parts of their body). Survivors of all genders also find too that they experience strong negative emotions in relation to specific parts of their bodies as a result of their experience(s) of sexual violence. For transgender survivors, their relationships with their bodies can be particularly complex. As a result, professionals working with them can unintentionally cause additional pain by relating to a survivor's body in ways which increase dysphoria or elicit strong negative emotional responses.

The language used to describe specific body parts can be very important in supporting transgender survivors. Again, it is best to simply be led by the language which the individual survivor (with whom you are working) wishes you to use. One survivor described to us a particularly good experience saying, 'They were brilliant. They asked me what language I wanted to use to refer to my body, what language I was comfortable with, and then just stuck to using that language... They made sure my body was referred to in ways I felt comfortable with' (Rymer and Cartei 2015, p.160). Another survivor spoke of their fear that being forced to use anatomical terms to describe their body would increase their sense of dysphoria, 'As a trans man, I would have to use terminology for my genitals that is incredibly painful and dysphoria-inducing in order to explain what he did to me' (Rymer and Cartei 2015, p.158). Survivors should be invited to freely choose what words are used to describe their body.

Because of the strong gender dysphoria that many transgender people experience in relation to parts of their body, it must also be an option for them to simply not discuss the physical realities of the violence they experienced or the effects of this on their body (or on their relationship with their body). As with any survivor, it may take trans survivors a very long time to be able to connect to the physical reality of what they have experienced. Rushing this or continually suggesting that transgender survivors engage in therapeutic conversations or exercises which aim to reconnect with or reclaim their bodies could lead the survivor to feel unsafe and not understood. This work can be valuable if undertaken in the right way and at the right time for the individual, but it should never be rushed.

Examining and treating bodies

Practitioners who as part of their work need to physically examine or touch a survivor's body (for example doctors, nurses or bodywork practitioners) should always use extra care and sensitivity when working with transgender survivors. Many transgender survivors will experience significant anxiety, dysphoria or discomfort before, during or after physical examinations or treatments. This is particularly true if these examinations or treatments focus on areas of the body that are associated with the survivors' gender dysphoria and/or their experience of sexual violence, or if the examination or procedure is invasive.

Some of these negative emotions can be managed by ensuring that patients have a chance to discuss in detail with their practitioner, ahead of any examination or treatment, what they might find difficult and how this can be managed. Survivors can be encouraged to use simple relaxation techniques before or during procedures to manage distress, and practitioners can assist them in doing so. With any survivor, it is important to have a detailed conversation prior to any examination or treatment, explaining exactly what will happen (keeping in mind that you should use a patient's preferred terminology to describe specific body parts).

It is always essential to ask consent throughout any physical examination or procedure and keep patients informed about what you are doing. Whenever possible, patients should be given the option to decline specific parts of the examination or treatment if those elements are not comfortable for them. It is also essential that patients are able to end an examination or procedure at any point if they are no longer able to tolerate it.

Consideration should also be given to how you can allow the survivor to be as 'in control' of the examination or treatment as possible. For example, would it be clinically acceptable for a patient to insert a swab or ultrasound wand themselves?

The privacy of transgender survivors must always be respected and survivors should never be expected to allow extra people (for example, students) into their room during an examination or procedure. It is also better for practitioners to refrain from making comments on a patient's gender presentation, even if those comments are intended to be positive (for example, 'The surgeon did a very good job with your gender reassignment surgery' or 'Those hormones are really working well'). Such comments may be experienced by the patient as you passing judgement on their body or their gender and these comments are also not likely to be relevant to the treatment or examination you are providing.

Physical examinations or procedures are often difficult for transgender individuals and for sexual violence survivors of any gender, but ensuring that the survivor is as informed, involved and respected as possible can go a long way in reducing this distress.

Working with highly complex individuals

Many services for survivors of sexual violence are experienced in supporting complex individuals. You probably already support a large diversity of survivors, many of whom will have multiple support needs and face multiple forms of oppression. For example, you may already have experience supporting survivors who face both mental health problems and physical disabilities or survivors who are asylum-seeking people of colour and of a minority religion. In common with these other groups, transgender survivors are also frequently individuals with complex identities and complex support needs.

As outlined earlier in this book, trans individuals often experience oppression and discrimination in many areas of their lives and as a result are disadvantaged and marginalised in complex ways. Given that transgender survivors so often face a range of other difficulties apart from their experience(s) of sexual violence, it is vital that professionals engage with them in such a way that recognises the complexity of their needs. For example, many survivors would find it very difficult to engage in trauma-focused therapeutic work when they are facing potential homelessness. Thus, supporters need to be prepared to offer transgender survivors support, or at the very least appropriate signposting to support, around the range of difficulties which they face.

While these complex intersections of oppression and discrimination bring much pain and many challenges, the experience of living through such difficulties also often means that transgender survivors have incredible resilience and hard-won strength in the face of overwhelming difficulty. This should be recognised, supported and enhanced by professionals who are working with them.

Navigating gendered services

Transgender survivors are also likely to need assistance in navigating the gendered services which are very common in the sexual violence recovery field. A large portion of such services are delivered exclusively to either men or women. For some transgender individuals who identify with a binary gender (i.e. trans men and trans women) these services may be suitable so long as they are safe for transgender individuals of the gender which they serve. But for other transgender individuals, such as non-binary people, this way of setting up services can create significant problems. It can create clear barriers to access, such as when non-binary survivors are excluded from the service criteria due to their gender. It can also create more subtle but no less harmful barriers, such as when non-binary survivors use a single-gender service because it is the only one available to them but find that they need to suppress or ignore a significant part of their identity in order to access the service. It may fall to you to assist survivors in navigating this network of services.

Unfortunately, there are no easy answers about how to help transgender survivors find services which can meet their needs and which would be open to and accessible for them. It is always best to be guided by the needs and preferences of the individual with whom you are working. Be honest with them about the service criteria of various organisations and offer to have a conversation with staff in the organisations about how they would ensure your client could safely access their service. It should never be suggested to a survivor that they use a service which does not correspond to their gender identity, but they should be informed of all their options. For example, if you are working with a non-binary survivor who was described as female at birth, this survivor should not simply be asked to use women-only services. Instead, you should explore all service options with them and endeavour to support them in accessing whatever service they decide best meets their needs.

This difficulty of finding appropriate services in a highly gendered service provision landscape is another reason why transgender survivors benefit from specialist services designed and run specifically for them. Unfortunately, such services are currently very rare. Those that do exist offer transgender survivors an opportunity to use much-needed services without having to worry about facing gender-related discrimination or having to fit themselves into a service that does not match their own gender identity. Such services can also offer survivors an opportunity to meet with others who have similar experiences to their own. As one survivor put it, '[I needed] services that either weren't gender specific or were for trans identified people. My experience and emotions surrounding the incest etc. are different from bio-males or bio-females. I didn't belong in any men's groups or women's groups' (a survivor quoted in munson and Cook-Daniels 2016, p.44).

In the next chapter, there is a fuller discussion of how the sexual violence recovery sector as a whole can move forward in considering and meeting the needs of non-binary survivors.

Key advice for therapeutic professionals

1. *Educate yourself on transgender identities.* Your client needs to know that you are able to understand them and that they will not have to hold the responsibility of teaching you about transgender identities. It is fine to sensitively ask questions about your client's gender identity, but be sure to have basic background information first. Chapter 1 of this book is a good place to start.

2. *Use your client's own words when talking about their identity or body.* It is essential that you clarify with your client early on

what words they would like used to describe their gender identity and various parts of their body. Use whatever words your client is comfortable with and only those words.

3. *Find ways of facilitating difficult discussions and disclosures.* Many clients will find it overwhelming or difficult to have initial conversations with you about their gender identity or trauma history. Find ways of making this initial information sharing less stressful for them, such as using the 'How best to support me' forms in the Appendix.

4. *Do not make any assumptions about 'links' between your client's gender identity and history of sexual trauma.* You should never make assumptions about any cause-and-effect relationship between your client's gender identity and their experience of sexual violence. It should never be assumed that they are transgender because of the sexual trauma they've experienced. They may have been targeted by their abuser specifically because of their gender identity, but their gender identity may also be completely unrelated to the circumstances in which they experienced sexual violence.

5. *Understand how gender dysphoria may interact with the way your client has experienced sexual trauma.* Dysphoria related to their body, particularly those areas of their body that do not align with their gender identity, is a common experience for many transgender people. Many transgender individuals will find ways of distancing themselves from the body parts which cause them the most distress. Because sexual violence often involves violence directed towards these body parts, connecting with or discussing the physical experiences related to their sexual trauma can be profoundly distressing for transgender survivors.

Key advice for independent sexual violence advocates

1. *Find ways of facilitating difficult discussions and disclosures.* Many clients will find it overwhelming or difficult to have initial conversations with you about their gender identity or trauma history. Find ways of making this initial information sharing less stressful for them, such as using the 'How best to support me' forms in the Appendix.

2. *Early on, discuss issues surrounding disclosures about your clients' gender identity.* Each client will have different needs and preferences around who in their case/support team needs to know about their gender identity. In some instances, this information will not need to be shared at all. If others involved in the client's case/support network do need information about your client's gender identity, the reasons for this should be clear and your client should always be consulted and have given consent before any information is shared. Clear expectations should be set for other professionals that they do the same.

3. *Assist in educating other professionals about transgender identities if your client would like you to do so.* It will likely be exhausting and distressing for your client to explain their gender identity to each professional involved in their case/support. Discuss with them if they would like you to support them in this as part of your advocacy role.

4. *Understand that 'outing' may be a major concern for your client, particularly if they are involved in a court case.* If your client's gender identity is likely to be discussed in court, your client may be concerned that this information could easily be spread. This may result in them being 'outed'

and potentially exposed to harassment, discrimination or further violence. If this is a concern, discuss with your client any measures which can be taken to keep information confidential.

5. *Share knowledge and best practice with other professionals.* As an independent sexual violence adviser, you probably have working relationships with a range of other professionals from a variety of backgrounds (such as police, legal, therapeutic and medical). Even before you have a transgender client, consider what you can do to support them to meet their needs.

Key advice for medical staff

1. *Consent is incredibly important during any physical examination.* Gaining consent before and during any physical examination is always best practice, but it may be even more important when working with transgender survivors. Before any physical examination, you should explain in detail what you will be doing and why you feel it is necessary. Check if all elements of the examination are okay with your patient or if they would rather you forgo or alter any elements of the examination. While you are undertaking the physical examination, let your patient know prior to touching or examining any new part of their body.

2. *Use your patient's own words when talking about specific body parts.* Check with your patient what words they would like you to use when referring to their body parts. Use the words they prefer when speaking to them, even if they are not the anatomically correct words. If you need to use other words

in your documentation, explain the reason for this to your patient and let them know what words will be used.

3. *Do not ask unnecessary questions.* Do not ask questions about your patient's body, gender transition or gender identity unless the questions are specifically related to the medical care you are providing. Your questions may come from a place of genuine interest and a desire to learn, but they may feel invasive or even hostile to your patient.

4. *Privacy is key.* Ensure that your patient is afforded as much privacy as possible. Any medical examination should take place in a private room with only essential staff, your patient and any support person they request. Their information should also be kept as private as possible and their gender identity or information about their body should not be disclosed to anyone without their consent.

5. *Do not comment on your patient's gender-related appearance.* Do not comment on your patient's physical transition or their gender-related appearance, even if you intend these comments to be complements (for example, 'Those hormones are really doing their job'). This may feel to your patient like yet another authority figure passing judgement on their body and gender identity.

Key advice for police and legal professionals

1. *Do not assume that non-disclosure about your client's gender identity is an attempt at deception.* The victim with whom you're working may not make any initial disclosures to you about their gender identity. This is likely not to be an attempt to withhold information but may be due to fear

of discrimination or simply the feeling that their gender identity is not an important factor in their experience of sexual violence.

2. *As much as possible, use your client's preferred name and pronoun as well as the words they prefer to use to describe parts of their body.* Clarify with your client early on what name they would prefer to be known by. Understand that they may use different names and pronouns in different circumstances and that these names and pronouns may not match their legal name or legal gender. Also check with them which words they would like used to describe their gender identity and any parts of their body which you might need to discuss. Use whatever words your client is comfortable with whenever possible. If there are instances when you must use their legal name or anatomical words to describe specific body parts, explain to them why this is.

3. *Understand that 'outing' may be a major concern for your client, particularly if they are involved in a court case.* If your client's gender identity is likely to be discussed in court, your client may be concerned that this information could easily be spread. This may result in them being 'outed' and potentially exposed to harassment, discrimination or further violence. If this is a concern, discuss with your client any measures that can be taken to keep information confidential.

4. *Do not make assumptions about the role your client's gender identity played in their experience of sexual trauma.* The violence experienced by your client may well have been a hate crime. They may have been targeted because of their gender identity. But do not make this assumption automatically. Their gender identity may not have anything to do with the circumstances around the assault.

5. *Understand that your client may have significant mistrust of the criminal justice system.* Due to previous experiences of discrimination, oppression and violence, many transgender people have significant mistrust of professional services. This is particularly true of the criminal justice system, which has a long history of violence towards the transgender community, including both violence directed at individuals and systemic discrimination (such as the practice of housing transgender prisoners in prisons that do not match their gender identity, and the lack of adequate healthcare provision for transgender individuals in prison).

Conclusion

This chapter has focused on how to support all survivors of sexual violence, with a particular focus on the needs of trans survivors. All survivors need a supportive, empathetic and non-judgemental attitude from all professionals who provide support. Trans survivors need professionals who find ways to quickly establish trust and who ensure that survivors know there will be no assumptions made about connections between the survivors' gender identity and their experience(s) of sexual trauma. They will also need practitioners who treat or discuss their bodies to take care in doing so and to always ensure they are being respectful and guided by the survivor. Trans survivors may require advice or advocacy too as they attempt to navigate a highly gendered service provision landscape. As with all survivors, trans survivors deserve support from profess-ionals who value them individually and work hard to meet their particular needs.

Chapter 7
Looking Ahead

Introduction

In this chapter, we look at the future of all service provision for trans and non-binary survivors. In doing so, we particularly focus on the role of the LGBT+ community and specialist sexual violence organisations. We begin by considering the pros and cons that characterise current service provision within those contexts. We then move on to make specific recommendations for improvement: a move to self-identification as the access criteria for gendered services; a shift from gender-neutral to all-gender service provision for services that are, or wish to be, not only serving a single gender; a recognition of the need for specialist services for trans survivors; and a closer collaboration between LGBT+ and sexual violence services. Through this discussion, we hope to contribute to individuals' and organisations' considerations about how they can think about and work with gender in a more modern and inclusive way, particularly when considering the needs of trans and non-binary survivors.

The role of the LGBT+ community

Several characteristics make LGBT+ organisations particularly well suited to support trans survivors. Trans people may already be accessing LGBT+ services and they may find these services more welcoming and sensitive than mainstream support services. Compared to mainstream services, LGBT+ services often, although by no means always, possess an increased level of awareness about transgender identities as well as the violence and oppression experienced by transgender people. Additionally, such organisations may be more accustomed to and accepting of individuals who present in an androgynous or gender diverse way. All of this can help to create an environment in which trans survivors feel safer and more understood.

Transgender people may of course also be lesbian, gay, bisexual or any other sexual orientation. In an LGBT+ organisation they are likely to find more acceptance around this as opposed to mainstream services, where they may be presumed to be heterosexual or where their gender identity and their sexual orientation could be conflated or confused. Again, this increased awareness and sensitivity can contribute to a safer environment for transgender survivors who wish to access support.

While some LGBT+ organisations have been working for a very long time to support transgender members of their community, it is also true that many LGBT+ organisations have a long history of forgetting or excluding transgender people. Many LGBT+ organisations have focused on the lesbian, gay and bisexual members of their community and neglected the needs of trans people. They may have focused their campaigning efforts on issues which affect LGB individuals (such as same-sex marriage and gay parenting rights) while ignoring other issues such as the violence faced by the trans community or inadequate access to healthcare for transgender individuals. Because of this history, trans people may feel let down by LGBT+ organisations. When this is the case, it will be important that organisations attempt to rebuild trust with the trans community by taking a wide interest in supporting the well-being of local trans people and by involving trans people in all levels of their organisation.

Another limitation of LGBT+ organisations that wish to support trans survivors of sexual violence is that they may have limited experience of working with survivors of sexual violence. Many LGBT+ organisations offer a broad range of support services which can include social groups, campaigning work around political issues, general well-being support and so on. Such organisations are unlikely to hold the organisational knowledge about trauma and gender-based violence that is common in specialist sexual violence services such as Rape Crisis Centres, though there are exceptions, such as the London-based, anti-violence charity Galop (Galop 2017). Staff and volunteers at LGBT+ organisations are also less likely to have access to the clinical supervision which forms an important part of supporting staff and volunteers at most sexual violence recovery organisations. This is not to say that LGBT+ organisations cannot build these capacities, but in order to deliver a safe and effective service they should plan to address these needs. One way to do so would be to deliver a service in partnership with an established sexual violence recovery service such as a Rape Crisis Centre. Partnerships such as these will be discussed later in this chapter.

Specialist sexual violence services

With the term 'specialist sexual violence services' we refer to those services whose core function is to support survivors of any kind of sexual violence, and whose workers have the skills and expertise to offer such tailored support. Most specialist services are run by voluntary sector organisations although some, such as sexual assault referral centres (SARCs), exist in the statutory sector. SARCs were first established in the UK in the 1980s in order to improve services for those who have experienced sexual violence, with an emphasis on high-quality and consistent forensic examinations. They have the dual aim of meeting both the medical and support needs of victims and the evidential needs of the criminal justice system. Voluntary sector organisations, such as Rape Crisis Centres, typically offer longer-term support and a more comprehensive range of services than SARCs to survivors and their families, such as helplines, email support, face-to-face support, groups, advocacy and accompaniment to health, police or court appointments, combined with awareness-raising and preventative work (for example, campaigning, training, education and consultancy).

Specialist sexual violence services often need to meet strict standards (for example, the Rape Crisis National Service Standards (Rape Crisis England & Wales and Rape Crisis Scotland 2012) and Quality Standards for Services Supporting Male Victims/ Survivors of Sexual Violence (Male Survivors Partnership 2018)) (LimeCulture 2017)), which intend to recognise the specific needs of survivors of sexual violence and benchmark the specialisms needed to provide services. These are informed by survivors' experience and based on research and consultation. The standards aim to ensure that all survivors receive a quality service regardless of their location, and also provide necessary evidence of service standards to funders.

Specialist sexual violence services, particularly voluntary organisations such as Rape Crisis Centres, are internationally recognised to be the most responsive to the needs of survivors, as acknowledged by the Council of Europe minimum standards (Kelly and Dubois 2008). A recent review of the relevant existing literature shows that specialisation brings particular benefits (Henderson 2012). At the core, these services are survivor-centred – they place power and control back in the hands of the individual who has experienced sexual violence, prioritising their rights, needs and wishes. They offer safety, holistic support, both short term and long term, for a whole range of sexual violence and abuse experiences across an individual's lifetime, while often non-specialist services and statutory services tend to focus on recent rape or sexual assault, and on the medical model, which pathologises individuals. They work alongside survivors to help them make decisions about how and where their healing process takes place. As a result, specialist services successfully reach survivors that other services do not reach. Moreover, while survivors using specialist services consistently report improved outcomes to their health and well-being, 'where there is no specialist provision many victim-survivors experience secondary victimisations and poor practice; the majority of reported cases are not prosecuted; many do not receive complete medical care; and most do not have access to quality mental health or support services' (Brown *et al.* 2010, in Henderson 2012).

Besides empowering individuals, specialist services play an essential role in promoting social change (Westmarland and Gangoli 2012). Lobbying government and running awareness and myth-busting campaigns are only some examples of the valuable work that these services do. They also play a key role in holding mainstream and statutory services accountable, which is largely due to maintaining at least some level of financial independence from the state. Indeed, US research on Rape Crisis Centres shows that where there is a centre, the community is more responsive to systemic efforts to address sexual violence (Schmitt and Martin 2006, in Henderson 2012).

Single-sex services

Historically, most specialist services have been grassroots organisations run by women for women in recognition that rape and other forms of sexual violence against women are crimes of violence and abuses of power that are rooted in gender-based inequalities, and which are used to perpetuate such inequalities. These organisations recognise the need to address the unique pressures and issues of inequality that women face within a patriarchal society. There is a strong body of evidence showing that women from all backgrounds generally feel safer in women-only services. Perceived safety in women-only contexts relates to freedom from physical harm, based on the fact that sexual violence is mostly perpetrated by men, leaving women more vulnerable in mixed-sex settings. There is also an increase in perceived safety from emotional harm, in that women are free from the gendered realities of daily public and private life, where women's experiences of objectification, silence and patriarchal judgement are routinely normalised (Women's Resource Centre 2010). Women also often report that sharing their own experiences and seeing other women at different stages of their healing journey supporting one another can be very empowering (Women's Resource Centre 2007).

Unlike specialist women-only services, which largely stemmed from the anti-rape movement of the 1960s and 70s, men-only services are often the projects of driven, highly committed individuals (Sullivan 2011). As with women-only organisations, men-only organisations strive to meet the unique needs of the survivors they serve. For example, because rape and sexual abuse are crimes traditionally associated with women as the victims, many male victims feel that they are the only person it has happened to, or that it happened to them because there is something wrong with them as a man. Male survivors of sexual violence also face specific myths in the context of society's expectations of 'masculinity' (for example, men should be able to protect themselves), their possible physiological reaction to the abuse (for example, erection or ejaculation means they experienced pleasure) and sexual identity (for example, sexual violence is only perpetrated against gay men, by gay men; men cannot be assaulted by women).

There is a need for further research about male victims to increase our understanding in this area, as Sullivan points out:

> Historically counselling for sexual abuse has been aimed at women using models that have been developed out of structural feminist theory. These address the unique pressures and issues of inequality that women face within a patriarchal society. For men, there is no such history of comprehensive research and co-ordinated response to develop a model of service delivery. (Sullivan 2011, p.3)

Sex versus self-identified gender

The gender-specific nature of many sexual violence recovery services has been a long-valued and incredibly useful aspect of these services. Given this, many such services are still grappling with understanding the role of trans survivors within their sector. Most single-gender services which aim to be inclusive of transgender survivors are open to all survivors who self-identify as the gender which the service aims to support (for example, a women's service would be open to all self-identifying women, which would include trans women). Some single-gender services are concerned that making this shift may open up their service to potential misuse from cisgender individuals of the other sex. As Rebecca Reilly-Cooper writes in regard to services providing support on the basis of self-declared gender identity:

> There is nothing to prevent this from being exploited and abused by men who, for a variety of reasons, may want access to services and protections that are currently provided to women on the basis of sex, not gender identity. This is not to say that trans people represent a threat to women, or that trans people want to abuse services and provisions made available for women. What it does mean is that when gender is entirely a matter of self-declaration, there is no way, either in principle or in practice, to distinguish genuine trans women from men who declare themselves women for the purposes of gaining access to women's spaces and availing themselves of women's resources... As long as special provisions are made for women, there will be at least some men who will want access to those provisions. For such men, making legally recognised gender a matter of mere self-declaration is a gift. (Reilly-Cooper 2016)

To this concern, we would respond that this issue is not one that emerges only when a service becomes open to all self-identifying people of one gender – it is an issue that could be faced by any single-gender service regardless of how it thinks about the boundaries around sex and gender. For example, no single-sex service asks all potential service users to 'prove' their sex prior to accessing the services. The only two ways to do so would be to ask potential service users to either submit documentation (such as a birth certificate) as evidence of their sex or to undergo some form of physical examination. The latter would obviously be entirely inappropriate in any circumstance and even more so in a service that supports survivors of sexual violence. In a women-only service, to ask for documentation would likely be successful in preventing cisgender men from accessing services, but it would also prevent any trans woman who had not yet changed her documentation from accessing the services.

Making changes in documentation is a long and difficult process, so this type of requirement would negatively affect many trans women. Trans women who have made changes to their legal documentation, however, would be able to utilise the service, and in this way requiring documentation would not be successful at ensuring the service was provided on the basis of 'sex at birth' rather than gender. Relying on documentation alone would also enable trans men (those who were described as female at birth but who have now transitioned) to access women's services if their documentation had not yet changed. Clearly such a policy put into practice would not succeed in drawing clear boundaries around who could and who couldn't access the service. Additionally, implementing such a system would create a huge amount of extra administrative work and slow down the process of accessing services for all survivors, particularly for drop-in or helpline services. Even if organisations are adamant that they want to restrict access to their services based on service users' sex at birth, there is no respectful and plausible way to do this in practice.

What most single-sex services currently rely on to draw boundaries around who can and who can't access a service is not truly a process by which they restrict access to services based on sex. Rather, they restrict access to services either based on individuals determining for themselves that a service is or is not for them, or based on staff and volunteers' perceptions of an individual's gender presentation. For example, if a cisgender man tried to access a women-only service, he would be turned away not because he could not provide documentation to prove his sex but because staff or volunteers 'knew' he was a man based on his appearance (or in the case of helplines, his tone of voice). This system relies on staff and volunteers judging the genders of other people and determining access to services based on these assumptions. With the increasing social acceptance of women and men presenting in more gender diverse ways, such a system is very vulnerable to misunderstanding.

No service would want to be in a position where they had to give volunteers or staff guidance on how to determine someone's gender based on how they presented (for example, she has long hair, has breasts or wears a dress and is therefore a woman); but without such guidance, these judgements would be down to individuals to make on their own. This system, if robustly enforced; would succeed in excluding many cisgender men, but it would also risk excluding many butch or masculine-presenting women. Additionally, it would put each staff member and volunteer in the vulnerable or uncomfortable position of having to potentially make a judgement about someone else's gender. Therefore, relying on the gender presentation or perceived gender of potential service users to determine who can or cannot access a service is similarly unlikely to produce the desired effect or be workable in practice.

Another concern that some individuals and organisations have about single-sex services being available to trans individuals is the belief that because trans individuals were generally not socialised as members of their self-identified gender from birth, it would not be appropriate for them to be in a space intended for individuals who have experienced sexual violence as members of that gender. For example, some are concerned that trans women will not have experienced patriarchy *as women* throughout their lifetime. There may be concern that a trans woman will have experienced male privilege during a period of her life when she was perceived by others to be male. From this perspective, a key element of women-only services is providing spaces where women can be around other people who have experienced patriarchy as women.

While it may be true that a trans woman hasn't experienced patriarchy as a woman her entire life, it is also true that she will have in all likelihood experienced patriarchy as a woman since transitioning; and on top of that she will have experienced transphobia which, like misogyny, is also a form of gender-related violence. While her journey with gender-related violence and discrimination will have been somewhat different from that of most cisgender women, she will almost certainly still have experiences of gender-related violence and discrimination and therefore will be quite capable of relating to and respecting the similar experiences of cisgender women.

Women's services exist for many very valid reasons and there are reasonable concerns about how to protect these services so that women continue to have access to specialist services. Yet, the concern about the *possibility* of services being utilised by those for whom they are not intended must be balanced against the *reality* that the current situation often prohibits transgender individuals from safely and comfortably using these essential services. It is therefore our view that while same-gender services are valuable and should be protected, they should always be provided on the basis of gender self-identification rather than sex.

Non-binary individuals

Even in single-gender services that are fully inclusive of all who self-identify with that gender, the question still emerges of what (if any), role non-binary survivors should play within such services. Currently, non-binary survivors often 'fall through the cracks', unable to access any of the single-gendered services available to other survivors. How non-binary survivors fit within such services is a very complex question since each non-binary individual experiences their own gender in a very individual way and each person's individual gender presentation is perceived by others in many different ways as well. For example, a non-binary person may have experienced sexual violence as a highly gendered assault in a context in which they were assumed to be a woman, even if this is not how they self-identify. Because of this experience, there may be value for them in being able to be with other people who have also experienced sexual violence as someone perceived to be a woman.

Another non-binary person may have experienced sexual violence as a transphobic hate crime. Some non-binary people are generally presumed to be female, others male, and some are perceived by the majority of people with mere confusion over their gender. Because of all this, one non-binary person may feel that a single-gender service is the most helpful service for them while another may not feel that service to be the right fit at all. Because of this complex set of factors, it is not possible to make a single statement about how non-binary individuals 'fit' within single-gender services.

Beyond the questions of whether or not single-gender services are a good fit for individual non-binary people, there is also the reality that in some areas single-gender services are the only viable option for support. In these instances, non-binary people may feel pressured to not disclose or discuss their gender in an effort to avoid being potentially turned away from the service. Suppressing a significant part of one's identity in order to access a service is never a good foundation for healing. This is one of the many reasons that it is necessary for a wider range of support services to be available so that individuals are able to access the service they feel is most appropriate for them. This would include services that are well equipped to support non-binary survivors alongside survivors of other genders. Such services must make it clear in their advertising that non-binary people are welcome in their service in order for non-binary survivors to feel safe and confident accessing their services.

Looking ahead: some suggestions

All-gender services

While some specialist services are gender specific, there are also sexual violence support services that are open to all people regardless of their gender. These are often called gender-neutral services. Moreover, organisations offering more generic support, such as the police, health and social services, also offer services to all survivors regardless of their gender. It may seem that since these services do not exclude anyone on the basis of their gender, they should be accessible and safe for transgender (including non-binary) individuals.

Unfortunately, gender-neutral services are not necessarily a safe or effective solution for trans (including non-binary) people. Too often, these services still work within the gender binary assumption. This means that their gender-neutral approach really means a 'men and women' approach, thereby overlooking those outside this binary. Hence, gender-neutral services should ensure that they are actively seen as 'all-gender' rather than 'gender-neutral' services, recognising and celebrating gender diversity at all levels of their organisation, as mentioned in previous chapters. Such an approach would bring back into these services a recognition that their service users' genders may affect their experience of the service. This would be valuable for trans and non-binary individuals, but also for cisgender individuals whose gender does impact the way they have experienced sexual violence.

Effective all-gender service provision does not necessarily mean offering the same to everyone – even within the gender binary, men and women's needs often differ, as do their experiences of sexual violence. The same is true for trans and non-binary survivors. For example, a trans person may experience sexual violence as part of a wider pattern of transphobic discrimination. Services that are open to all genders will still need to be gender-informed in their approach to service provision.

The financial pressure that providers are under to offer gender-neutral services seems motivated by commissioners' drive for lowest unit cost, rather than the provision of quality services that respect gender diversity. This must change if these services are to offer gender-informed services.

All-gender services that are gender-informed can focus on the common needs of all survivors while still considering how these needs might be affected by their users' genders.

A review of sexual abuse services in Fife gives an indication of what service users experiencing different forms of sexual violence are looking for (Reid Howie 2005). The kinds of support they wanted included: provision of safe space, general support, information, counselling, groupwork and opportunities to meet other survivors, telephone support, crisis support, practical support (for example with form filling), advocacy, befriending, liaison with other agencies, support to move on, and opportunities for outings and 'ordinary' events. All-gender services should continue offering these types of support to all their service users but they can offer the support in a way which is informed by considerations about gender. For example, as seen throughout this book, the provision of a safe space requires a lot of thought about gender for trans and non-binary survivors, but also for cisgender men and women. Groupwork can be successfully offered in all-gender contexts, but depending on the content of the sessions there may also be value in offering a range of groups including all-gender groups, trans groups, women's groups, men's groups and so on. With all types of support, services should consider how a service user's gender might affect the way they experience the support; and changes to the way services are delivered should be made in line with the responses to this issue.

Specialist services for trans and non-binary survivors

While other services and organisations certainly have a role in supporting trans and non-binary survivors of sexual violence, there is also a clear need for specialist services for transgender and non-binary survivors. All of the drawbacks discussed in the above sections can create barriers for trans survivors contemplating accessing support from universal services, single-gender services or LGBT+ services. These barriers are generally eliminated when specialist support can be offered directly to transgender (including non-binary) survivors rather than asking them to fit into pre-existing services. Additionally, a huge amount can be gained by offering trans and non-binary survivors a service which is entirely their own.

One of the major barriers faced by trans survivors wishing to access a service is the understandable fear that many trans people feel any time they access a new service. Given the level of discrimination and violence faced by trans people, including at the hands of 'helping professionals', the presumption that any service or organisation is unsafe until proven otherwise is quite reasonable. At times, the risk involved in approaching a support service can be too great. A specialist service designed for trans and non-binary survivors, especially if it is staffed by trans and non-binary staff and volunteers, is far more likely to feel both safe and approachable. Not only does this mean that the service is more likely to be utilised; it will also help create a vital feeling of safety within the service.

Such services can also open up the possibility of connecting with a collective or community who understand the survivor on a deep level. Many women-only sexual violence recovery services grew out of collectives of women who sought empowerment and healing together. There is incredible healing to be found within a community that has shared experiences and identities. Trans-specific services are much more likely to offer opportunities for trans people to work together to both access help and offer support to other members of their community.

In such a service, trans and non-binary survivors are more likely to trust that staff, volunteers and other survivors will 'get it' when they talk about their experiences. This is often the case in any specialist service targeted at individuals who have a shared identity or experience. In these services, individuals can trust that they will be understood and that they are less likely to need to explain key parts of their identity or experiences. Coincidentally, at the time we write this book, 'Me Too' has spread virally as a hashtag used on social media to both demonstrate the widespread prevalence of sexual assault and harassment, and empower women through empathy. This movement has illustrated how powerful it can be to find other survivors who share a common experience.

In these specialist services, trans people also do not need to worry about being the only trans or non-binary person using the service as they might in other less specialist services. With this comes a decrease in fear of being outed and a decrease in worries about potential transphobic responses from other service users, staff and volunteers. In our research about what trans survivors would like in a service, 64 per cent of participants said that it would be important or very important that they were not the only trans or non-binary person using the service (Rymer and Cartei 2015, p.160).

While there are major benefits to offering a specialist service for trans and non-binary survivors of sexual violence, there are also some drawbacks to be aware of. First, there is a risk that when sufficient specialist services exist for trans and non-binary survivors, other mainstream services will become less motivated to make changes which would help them to be safer and more accessible for trans and non-binary survivors. It is possible that when such specialist services exist, other services could become less concerned with trans survivors due to the assumption that they have their own dedicated service and therefore do not need the support of other organisations. Of course, what is missed in that assumption is that trans and non-binary survivors deserve (and indeed have a right) to have choice over which services they access. It is important to have specialist services for trans and non-binary survivors, but it is equally important that all services which work with survivors of sexual violence are equipped to offer a safe and accessible service to any trans or non-binary survivor who comes through their doors. The choice of which service they would like to use must ultimately lie with the survivor themselves. If the existence of specialist services leads mainstream services to be unconcerned about trans and non-binary survivors, these survivors will not experience any genuine choice over which services they utilise.

Another potential difficulty which specialist services may face is that in many areas the trans community is relatively small in numbers. This can create two problems: limited utilisation of the service, and many service users and staff and volunteers knowing each other personally. Both of these issues can be dealt with in the first instance by making services available to as wide a group of people as possible. For example, a helpline or online support forum can be made available to trans survivors nationally rather than only those in a particular town or region. This will both increase the number of people who are likely to utilise the service and decrease the likelihood of service users, staff and volunteers knowing each other personally. This second issue is not always a problem, but can become one if service users are concerned about either breaches in confidentiality or how their interactions with people within the service will impact their interactions with these same individuals in social settings. Some of these concerns can be minimised with clear confidentiality policies which are easily accessible to all, but this dynamic may require careful and proactive management.

It is also possible that in specialist services for trans and non-binary survivors, both victims and perpetrators may be part of the same small community and may wish to access services if both have been victims of sexual violence at some point in their lifetime. This too requires careful and thoughtful management, with the focus always remaining on ensuring a sense of safety and of being valued and believed for as many service users as possible. It can be useful to have multiple ways in which survivors can access support so that individuals are still able to access some form of support even if it is not possible for them to access other types of support. For example, the organisation may conclude that a particular service user is not able to access a drop-in service, but counselling and helpline support may still be available to them.

Another aspect of such services which needs to be carefully managed is quality assurance. Sexual violence recovery services for women are guided by the Rape Crisis England & Wales National Service Standards (Rape Crisis England & Wales and Rape Crisis Scotland 2012), and a similar set of standards are currently being developed for services which cater to men (LimeCulture 2017). These guidelines provide benchmarks which help to confirm that all organisations in the sector provide a quality service. These shared standards also enable opportunities for co-ordination between organisations, information and knowledge sharing, and mutual support. Trans-specific services would need to consider how they will ensure their services meet relevant standards and what new standards may need to be introduced in order to confirm the services are meeting the needs of their particular service users. The existing Rape Crisis England & Wales National Service Standards and the forthcoming standards from LimeCulture could be a good starting point for the development of such trans-specific standards.

Another potential issue to consider is that, from our own experience, securing funding for specialist services for trans and non-binary survivors can also be very difficult. The current funding environment for sexual violence recovery services privileges services that are directed to either men or women. Many such grants come with the stipulation that they are for 'women-only services' or 'men-only services'. At the time of writing, there is no grant funding available that specifically aims to enhance service provision for transgender survivors. Therefore, specialist services such as these may need to look further afield for potential funding sources. At the same time, it is vital that funders consider the implications for trans and non-binary survivors of so much of the available funding being targeted at binary-gendered services.

The final potential drawback to consider with creating specialist services for trans and non-binary survivors of sexual violence is finding the proper balance between suitably specialist services and overly specialised services which target such a specific and narrow group of service users that uptake of the service is likely to be quite low. Each area and each service is unique, so there are no hard and fast rules to determine if a service is overly specialised to the point of being unlikely to draw enough service users. For example, some Rape Crisis Centres have found great success in running specialist groups or workshops for BME survivors, but others have attempted this and have not experienced a high enough turnout to continue with the service. Many factors can influence this outcome and they should all be considered while making the decision to set up a specialised service. Organisations should: assess the need for such a service and scope out the likely number of potential service users in their local area; ask potential service users what kinds of services they would like; and consider if they have sufficient links and good enough relationships with their target community to ensure that the message about this new service would reach those who would benefit from knowing about it. If the organisation is not able to find answers to any of these issues, they may first need to build stronger links with their target community and undertake a scoping exercise to gain the views from this community about the necessity of the proposed service as well as how it can best be run.

Collaboration between LGBT organisations and sexual violence services

Survivors of sexual violence have unique needs which benefit from a unique service, but there is also scope for collaboration. No one agency can address all survivors' needs, so it makes sense for agencies to work together for the benefit of survivors generally. Some organisations have already proved successful in offering ways in which their services and expertise can be 'fruitfully combined'. One such example is the Trans Survivors Switchboard helpline, the first UK helpline to offer support to trans people (including those who are non-binary and questioning their gender identity) who have experienced sexual violence at any point in their lifetime. Jointly run by Brighton & Hove LGBT Switchboard (a specialist LGBT+ organisation) and the Survivors Network Rape Crisis Centre in Sussex, the helpline is staffed by trans and non-binary volunteers.

The decision to use only trans and non-binary volunteers was made following our research in which over half (56%) of trans survivors said that it was important or very important that the sta and volunteers at the service they wish to use are also trans or non-binary (Rymer and Cartei 2015, p.160). These volunteers have received training from these organisations and developed knowledge and skills in both working with survivors of sexual violence and supporting LGBT+ individuals. To this partnership, Survivors Network has brought a specialism in supporting survivors of sexual violence, while LGBT Switchboard has brought a well-established relationship with the local LGBT+ community and a depth of knowledge and skills about the support needs of LGBT+ individuals.

This partnership has enabled the delivery of a service that neither organisation could provide on its own. For survivors, it has meant that they are able to access a service that understands two important aspects of their identity: their gender and their survivorhood. One survivor commented that the service is the only place where they could 'talk about that exact nuanced problem and feel completely understood'. Another survivor said, 'It's a real relief to just have a space to rant about the intricacies of being an abuse victim/survivor and a trans person. And to just have someone who is understanding. This service is a real relief, a place to breathe, and I feel like a set of complex problems I have going on are best understood here, on this helpline.' While it is essential that single-gender and all-gender service providers also ensure that trans and non-binary survivors are able to safely access their services, these comments from trans survivors demonstrate just how necessary specialist services for trans and non-binary survivors really are. Very often, these types of services can be effectively delivered via a partnership between LGBT+ organisations and sexual violence recovery organisations.

Conclusion

Sexual violence recovery services exist across a variety of sectors and are run in rich and varied ways. Many of these services arose out of the feminist movements in the 1960s and 70s and these services have been supporting women survivors very effectively for decades. More recently, specialist services have emerged for men who have survived sexual violence. Gender-neutral services are increasingly offered by statutory services and some voluntary agencies. Within this service provision landscape, trans survivors are far too often ignored or excluded.

There are a number of ways to improve professionals' support for trans survivors. We have suggested that single-gender services should always use self-identification of one's gender as their access criteria rather than focusing on someone's sex. The gender-neutral services that do exist should give more consideration to the impact of users' genders on their experiences of sexual violence and of using the service. By doing so, they can move towards being 'all-gender' services rather than 'gender-neutral' services. In addition to these changes to existing services, specialist services for trans and non-binary survivors are also needed in order to ensure they have a full range of support options, including services where they know they will be supported by and among people who are also trans. By making these changes, we can all contribute to the healing and recovery of trans and non-binary individuals who have experienced sexual violence.

Appendix

In this appendix, you will find three 'How best to support me' documents. These can be copied and utilised in day-to-day practice. These, or similar written questions, offer trans survivors an opportunity to let you know in writing how you can best support them.

How best to support me: medical appointment

This paper is aimed at providing you with information that will help us work together so that I can get what I need out of this appointment. Relating to my gender identity, there are some things I would like you to know before we start the appointment. Please see below:

My name and the pronouns I use: ....

....

What I'd like to get out of this appointment: ....

....

What, if anything, you need to know about my gender identity: ....

....

....

What, if anything, you need to know about my body: ....

....

....

What terms I'd like you to use to refer to parts of my body: ....

....

....

Any parts of my body I do not want to discuss with you: ....

....

....

Any parts of my body you do not have my consent to examine or touch: .....

....

....

Any other information: ....

....

How best to support me: police or legal appointment

This paper is aimed at providing you with information that will help us work together so that I can get what I need out of this appointment. Relating to my gender identity, there are some things I would like you to know before we start the appointment. Please see below:

My name and the pronouns I use: ....

....

What I'd like to get out of this appointment: ....

....

What, if anything, you need to know about my gender identity: ....

....

What, if anything, you need to know about my body: ....

....

What terms I'd like you to use to refer to parts of my body: ....

....

Any parts of my body I do not want to discuss with you: ....

....

Concerns I have about my involvement with the police and potential legal action:

....

....

My expectations around disclosure about my gender identity to people within your service (i.e. other police officers or solicitors): ....

....

My expectations around disclosure about my gender identity to people outside your service (i.e. the press, judges, a jury and so on): ....

....

Any other information: ....

How best to support me: therapeutic appointment

This paper is aimed at providing you with information that will help us work together so that I can get what I need out of this appointment. Relating to my gender identity, there are some things I would like you to know before we start the appointment. Please see below:

My name and the pronouns I use: ....

....

What I'd like to get out of this appointment: ....

....

What, if anything, you need to know about my gender identity: ....

....

....

What, if anything, you need to know about my body: ....

....

....

What terms I'd like you to use to refer to parts of my body: ....

....

....

Any parts of my body I do not want to discuss with you: ....

....

....

Any assumptions you should NOT make about connections between my gender identity and experience(s) of sexual violence:.....................

....

....

Any other information: ....

Glossary of Terms

Agender: Someone who identifies as being 'without a gender'.

Cisgender: Someone who is not transgender.

Coming out: The gradual process of disclosing to other people one's gender identity. For most trans people this is not something which happens once and then is done, but rather a gradual process of disclosure to various people (such as family, friends) and institutions (such as banks, GP surgeries, employers, schools). This process may continue for years after someone transitions.

Gender: A culturally dictated set of rules, boundaries and norms which dictate expectations about how individuals behave, present and understand themselves based on the gender categories relevant to that culture (such as male, female, two-spirit).

Gender dysphoria: Distress caused by incongruences between one's own gender identity and the gender-related assumptions that others make about you; gender-related distress caused by one's primary or secondary sexual characteristics.

Gender fluid: A gender identity in which someone does not identify as having one fixed gender.

Gender identity: One's own personal perception and experience of one's gender.

Genderqueer or non-binary: A broad term for anyone whose gender identity lies between or beyond the binary genders.

Queer: A very broad term which is often used to be inclusive of all members of the LGBT+ community.

Sex: A medical classification (generally male, female or intersex) used to describe one's primary and secondary sexual characteristics as well as one's genetics.

Stealth: Someone who has transitioned and now generally chooses not to disclose their gender history.

Transition: A series of social, medical, physical and legal processes by which someone moves from one gender to another gender. There is no one path for a gender transition and each individual will choose, for a variety of reasons, which processes to undertake and which not to undertake.

Trans man: Someone whose body was assigned female at birth but who identifies as a man. Sometimes abbreviated as FtM (female to male).

Trans woman: Someone whose body was assigned male at birth but who identifies as a woman. Sometimes abbreviated MtF (male to female).

References

Afifi, T.O. and MacMillan, H.L. (2011) 'Resilience following child maltreatment: A review of protective factors.' *Canadian Journal of Psychiatry*, 56, 5, 266–272.

Anda, R.F., Felitti, V.J., Bremner, J.D., Walker, J.D. *et al.* (2006) 'The enduring effects of abuse and related adverse experiences in childhood.' *European Archives of Psychiatry and Clinical Neuroscience*, 256, 3, 174–186.

Balzer, C. and Hutta, J.S. (2012) *Transrespect vs Transphobia Worldwide*. Accessed on 28/12/17 at http://transrespect.org/wp-content/uploads/2015/08/TvT_research-report.pdf.

Bariola, E., Lyons, A., Leonard, W., Pitts, M., Badcock, P. and Couch, M. (2015) 'Demographic and psychosocial factors associated with psychological distress and resilience among transgender individuals.' *American Journal of Public Health*, 105, 10, 2108–2116.

Bockting, W.O., Miner, M.H., Swinburne Romine, R.E., Hamilton, A. and Coleman, E. (2013) 'Stigma, mental health, and resilience in an online sample of the US transgender population.' *American Journal of Public Health*, 103, 5, 943–951.

Bonanno, G.A., Colak, D.M., Keltner, D., Shiota, M.N. *et al.* (2007) 'Context matters: The benefits and costs of expressing positive emotion among survivors of childhood sexual abuse.' *Emotion*, 7, 4, 824.

Browne, K., Scott, E.-J., Valentine, V. and Antoniou, M. (2015) *Trans Community Research Final Project Report*. Accessed on 05/01/2018 at www.bhconnected.org.uk/sites/bhconnected/files/ Brighton&Hove Trans Community Research Project 2015.pdf.

Center for American Progress and MAP (2016) *Unjust: How the Broken Criminal Justice System Fails Transgender People*. Washington, DC: Center for American Progress. Accessed on 04/10/17 at www.lgbtmap.org/file/lgbt-criminal-justice-trans.pdf.

Chambers, R. (1997) *Whose Reality Counts?* (Vol. 25). London: Intermediate Technology Publications.

Close the Gap (2017) *Statement in support of the Equal Recognition Campaign and reform of the Gender Recognition Act*, November. Accessed on 05/01/2018 at www.closethegap.org.uk/news/blog/ statement-in-support-of-the-equal-recognition-campaign-and-reform-of-the-gender-recognitio.

Dixon-Woods, M., Cavers, D., Agarwal, S., Annandale, E. *et al.* (2006) 'Conducting a critical interpretive synthesis of the literature on access to healthcare by vulnerable groups'. *BMC Medical Research Methodology*, 6, 1, 35.

Ehlers, A. (2010) 'Understanding and treating unwanted trauma memories in posttraumatic stress disorder.' *Zeitschrift für Psychologie/Journal of Psychology*, 218, 141–145.

Elliott, D.E., Bjelajac, P., Fallot, R.D., Markoff, L.S. and Reed, B.G. (2005) 'Trauma-informed or trauma-denied: Principles and implementation of trauma-informed services for women.' *Journal of Community Psychology*, 33, 4, 461–477.

Engender (2017) *Statement in support of the Equal Recognition Campaign and reform of the Gender Recognition Act*. Accessed on 05/01/2018 at www.engender.org.uk/news/blog/statement-in-support-of-the-equal-recognition-campaign-and-reform-of-the-gender-recognitio.

Equality Act 2010. Accessed on 05/01/2018 at www.legislation.gov. uk/ukpga/2010/15.

Estrella, M., Blauert, J., Campilan, D., Gaventa, J. *et al.* (2000) *Learning from Change: Issues and Experiences in Participatory Monitoring and Evaluation.* London: Practical Action Publishing, International Development Research Centre.

Faye, S. (2017) 'Trans women need access to rape and domestic violence services. Here's why.' *The Guardian*, 21 November. Accessed on 05/01/2018 at www.theguardian.com/ commentisfree/2017/nov/21/trans-women-rape-domestic-violence-dangers.

Frazier, P., Conlon, A. and Glaser, T. (2001) 'Positive and negative life changes following sexual assault.' *Journal of Consulting and Clinical Psychology*, 69, 6, 1048.

Gallagher, A. (2017) 'No, transgender women like me did not grow up with "male privilege".' *Sydney Morning Herald*, 14 March. Accessed on 07/04/18 at: https://www.smh.com.au/lifestyle/ no-transgender-women-like-me-did-not-grow-up-with-male-privilege-20170314-guxhth.html.

Galop (2017) *How We Can Help.* Accessed on 21/01/18 at www.galop. org.uk/how-we-can-help.

GenderTrender (2014) *Reclaim The March! Statement from Radical Feminists on what occurred at London Reclaim The Night 2014.* Accessed on 05/01/2018 at https://gendertrender.wordpress. com/2014/11/24/reclaim-the-march-statement-from-radical-feminists-on-what-occurred-at-london-reclaim-the-night-2014.

Gosling, L. and Edwards, M. (2003) *Toolkits: A Practical Guide to Planning, Monitoring, Evaluation and Impact Assessment.* London: Save the Children UK.

Gottschalk, L.H. (2009) 'Transgendering women's space: A feminist analysis of perspectives from Australian women's services.' *Women's Studies International Forum*, 23, 167–178.

Grant, J., Mottet, L., Tanis, J., Harrison, J., Herman, J. and Keisling, K. (2011) *Injustice at Every Turn: A Report of the National Transgender Discrimination Survey*. Washington, DC: National Center for Transgender Equality and National Gay and Lesbian Task Force. Accessed on 03/10/17 at www.thetaskforce.org/static_html/downloads/reports/reports/ntds_full.pdf.

Griffiths, C., Gerressu, M. and French, R.S. (2008) 'Are one-stop shops acceptable? Community perspectives on one-stop shop models of sexual health service provision in the UK.' *Sexually Transmitted Infections*, 84, 5, 395–399.

Halliday, J. (2017) 'Transgender woman found dead in cell at Doncaster prison.' *The Guardian*, 5 January. Accessed on 28/12/2017 at www.theguardian.com/society/2017/jan/05/transgender-woman-jenny-swift-found-dead-at-doncaster-prison.

Henderson, S. (2012) 'The pros and cons of providing dedicated sexual violence services.' *Rape Crisis Scotland*. Accessed on 28/03/18 at www.rapecrisisscotland.org.uk/resources/SVservices-lit-review-1.pdf.

Hill, A. and Condon, R. (2015) *Brighton & Hove: Trans Needs Assessment*. Accessed on 21/01/18 at www.bhconnected.org.uk/sites/bhconnected/files/Brighton & Hove Trans Needs Assessment 2015.pdf.

Human Rights Campaign (2015) *Addressing Anti-Transgender Violence*. Human Rights Campaign. Accessed on 05/10/17 at www.hrc.org/resources/addressing-anti-transgender-violence-exploring-realities-challenges-and-sol.

Jacques-Tiura, A.J., Tkatch, R., Abbey, A. and Wegner, R. (2010) 'Disclosure of sexual assault: Characteristics and implications for posttraumatic stress symptoms among African American and Caucasian survivors.' *Journal of Trauma & Dissociation*, 11, 2, 174–192.

James, S.E., Herman, J.L., Rankin, S., Keisling, M., Mottet, L. and Anafi, M. (2016) *The Report of the 2015 U.S. Transgender Survey.* Washington, DC: National Center for Transgender Equality. Accessed on 03/10/17 at www.transequality.org/sites/default/files/docs/usts/USTS Full Report FINAL 1.6.17.pdf.

Kelly, L. and Dubois, L. (2008) *Combating Violence Against Women: Minimum Standards for Support Services.* Strasbourg: Council of Europe. Directorate General of Human Rights and Legal Affairs.

Kolk, B.A., Burbridge, J.A. and Suzuki, J. (1997) 'The psychobiology of traumatic memory.' *Annals of the New York Academy of Sciences*, 821, 1, 99–113.

LGBT Domestic Abuse Project (2015) *Stronger Together: Guidance for Women's Services on the Inclusion of Transgender Women.* The LGBT Domestic Abuse Project, Scottish Women's Aid, the Tayside Violence Against Women Training Consortium and the Scottish Transgender Alliance. Accessed on 05/10/17 at www.scottishtrans.org/wp-content/uploads/2016/05/Stronger_Together_-_September_2015.pdf.

Male Survivors Partnership (2018). *Male Service Standards.* Accessed on 01/08/2018 at http://www.malesurvivor.co.uk/male-service-standards.

MacLean, P.D. (1990) *The Triune Brain in Evolution: Role in Paleocerebral Functions.* New York: Plenum.

McNeil, J., Bailey, L., Ellis, S., Morton, J. and Regan, M. (2012) *Trans Mental Health Study*. Edinburgh: Scottish Transgender Alliance. Accessed on 03/10/17 at www.gires.org.uk/wp-content/uploads/2014/08/trans_mh_study.pdf.

Mukwege, D. and Berg, M. (2016) 'A holistic, person-centred care model for victims of sexual violence in Democratic Republic of Congo: The Panzi Hospital One-Stop Centre Model of Care.' *PLoS Medicine*, 13, 10.

munson, m. and Cook-Daniels, L. (2015) *Let's Talk About It! A Transgender Survivor's Guide to Accessing Therapy*. Forge. Accessed on 05/01/2018 at http://forge-forward.org/wp-content/docs/Lets-Talk-Therapist-Guide.pdf.

munson, m. and Cook-Daniels, L. (2016) *A Guide for Facilitators of Transgender Community Groups: Supporting Sexual Violence Survivors*. Forge. Accessed on 05/01/2018 at http://forge-forward.org/wp-content/docs/facilitators-guide-trans-support-groups.pdf.

Parks, W., Gray-Felder, D., Hunt, J. and Byrne, A. (2005) *Who Measures Change? An Introduction to Participatory Monitoring and Evaluation of Communication for Social Change*. South Orange, NJ: Communication for Social Change Consortium.

Pearlman, L.A. and Saakvitne, K.W. (1995) *Trauma and the Therapist: Countertransference and Vicarious Traumatization in Psychotherapy with Incest Survivors*. New York, NY: WW Norton & Co.

Phipps, A. (2014) *Why feminism needs trans people and sex workers*. Accessed on 21/01/18 at https://genderate.wordpress.com/2014/11/26/why-feminism-needs-trans-people-and-sex-workers.

Public Broadcasting Service (PBS) (2015) *A Map of Gender-Diverse Cultures*. Independent Television Service. Accessed on 02/10/17 at www.pbs.org/independentlens/content/two-spirits_map-html.

Rape Crisis England & Wales (2017a) *Why Women & Girls?* Accessed on 28/12/2017 at http://rapecrisis.org.uk/whywomengirls.php.

Rape Crisis England & Wales (2017b) *Working in the Sexual Violence Sector: Course Material*. (Accessed in the Rape Crisis Training programme, in the members' area.)

Rape Crisis England & Wales (2018) *What is Sexual Violence?* Accessed on 21/01/18 at https://rapecrisis.org.uk/sexualviolenceoverview.php.

Rape Crisis England & Wales and Rape Crisis Scotland (2012) *Rape Crisis National Service Standards: Summary Information for Partners, Funders and Commissioners*. Accessed on 05/01/2018 at https://rapecrisis.org.uk/userfiles/PDFs/RCNSS.pdf.

Rape Crisis Scotland (2011) *Stronger Together: Guidance for Women's Services on the Inclusion of Transgender Women*. Accessed on 05/01/2018 at www.rapecrisisscotland.org.uk/publications/single-sex-service-trans-guidance.pdf.

Reid Howie Associates (2005) *Sexual Abuse Services in Fife*. Edinburgh: Scottish Executive.

Reilly-Cooper, R. (2016) *Equality for Trans People Must Not Come at the Expense of Women's Safety*. Accessed on 05/01/2018 at www.politics.co.uk/comment-analysis/2016/01/26/equality-for-trans-people-must-not-come-at-the-expense-of-wo.

Resick, P.A. and Schnicke, M.K. (1992) 'Cognitive processing therapy for sexual assault victims.' *Journal of Consulting and Clinical Psychology*, 60, 5, 748–756.

Runtz, M.G. and Schallow, J.R. (1997) 'Social support and coping strategies as mediators of adult adjustment following childhood maltreatment.' *Child Abuse & Neglect*, 21, 2, 211–226.

Rymer, S. and Cartei, V. (2015) 'Supporting transgender survivors of sexual violence: Learning from users' experiences.' *Critical and Radical Social Work*, 3, 1, 155–164.

Sausa, L.A., Keatley, J. and Operario, D. (2007) 'Perceived risks and benefits of sex work among transgender women of color in San Francisco.' *Archives of Sexual Behavior*, 36, 6, 768–777.

Schein, L.A. (2006) *Psychological Effects of Catastrophic Disasters: Group Approaches to Treatment*. New York, NY: Haworth Press.

Siegel, D.J. (2001) 'Toward an interpersonal neurobiology of the developing mind: Attachment relationships, "mindsight", and neural integration.' *Infant Mental Health Journal*, 22, 1-2, 67–94.

Singh, A., Hays, D. and Watson, L. (2011) 'Strength in the face of adversity: Resilience strategies of transgender individuals.' *Journal of Counseling & Development*, 89, 1, 20–27.

Stonewall (2016) *Getting it Right with Your Trans Service Users and Customers*. Accessed on 05/10/17 at www.stonewall.org.uk/sites/default/files/getting_it_right_with_your_trans_service_users_and_customers.pdf.

Sullivan, M. (2011) *An Exploration of Service Delivery to Male Survivors of Sexual Abuse*. Accessed on 21/01/18 at www.wcmt.org.uk/sites/default/files/migrated-reports/840_1.pdf.

TransWhat? (2017) *Glossary of Terms*. Accessed on 02/10/17 at https://transwhat.org/glossary/#S.

Transgender Europe (2017) *Trans Rights Europe Map & Index 2017*. Accessed on 04/10/17 at https://tgeu.org/trans-rights-map-2017.

Turner, L., Whittle, S. and Combs, R. (2009) *Transphobic Hate Crime in the European Union*. London: Press for Change. Accessed on 04/10/17 at www.ilga-europe.org/sites/default/files/transphobic_hate_crime_in_the_european_union_0.pdf.

TvT research project (2015) *Trans Murder Monitoring*. Transrespect versus Transphobia Worldwide (TvT) project website. Accessed on 28/12/2017 at www.transrespect.org/en/research/trans-murder-monitoring.

Ullman, S.E. (1999) 'Social support and recovery from sexual assault: A review.' *Aggression and Violent Behavior*, 4, 3, 343–358.

Ungar, M. (ed.) (2012) *The Social Ecology of Resilience: A Handbook of Theory and Practice*. New York, NY: Springer.

Urquhart, E. (2015) *Women-Only Spaces Aren't Necessarily Safe Spaces*. December. Accessed on 05/01/2018 at www.slate.com/blogs/outward/2015/12/22/women_only_spaces_aren_t_necessarily_safe_spaces.html.

Valadez, J. and Bamberger, M. (1994) *Monitoring and Evaluating Social Programs in Developing Countries*. Washington, DC: Banco Mundial.

Valentine, L. and Feinauer, L.L. (1993) 'Resilience factors associated with female survivors of childhood sexual abuse.' *American Journal of Family Therapy*, 21, 3, 216–224.

Wasco, S. (2003) 'Conceptualizing the harm done by rape: Applications of trauma theory to experiences of sexual assault.' *Violence, Trauma & Abuse*, 4, 4, 309–322.

Westmarland, N. and Gangoli, G. (eds) (2012) *International Approaches to Rape*. Bristol: Policy Press.

Whittle, S., Turner, L., Combs, R. and Rhodes, S. (2008) *Transgender EuroStudy: Legal Survey and Focus on the Transgender Experience of Health Care*. Brussels: ILGA-Europe. Accessed on 28/12/2017 at www.pfc.org.uk/pdf/eurostudy.pdf.

Women's Resource Centre (2007) *Why Women Only? The Value and Benefits of By Women, For Women Services.* Accessed on 27/11/17 at https://thewomensresourcecentre.org.uk/wp-content/uploads/whywomenonly.pdf.

Women's Resource Centre (2010) *Women-only Services: Making the Case.* Accessed on 27/11/17 at https://thewomensresourcecentre.org.uk/wp-content/uploads/Making-the-case-for-women-only-July-2011.pdf.

World Health Organization (2017) *Gender, Equality and Human Rights.* Accessed on 02/10/17 at www.who.int/gender-equity-rights/understanding/gender-definition/en.

Xie, P., Kranzler, H.R., Poling, J., Stein, M.B. *et al.* (2009) 'Interactive effect of stressful life events and the serotonin transporter 5-HTTLPR genotype on posttraumatic stress disorder diagnosis in 2 independent populations.' *Archives of General Psychiatry*, 66, 11, 1201–1209.

Further Reading

General reading about supporting survivors of sexual violence

Ainscough, C. and Toon, K. (1993) *Breaking Free: Help for Survivors of Child Sexual Abuse*. London: Sheldon Press.

Bass, E. and Davis, L. (2002) *The Courage to Heal: A Guide for Women Survivors of Child Sexual Abuse*. New York, NY: Random House.

Kelly, L. (2013) *Surviving Sexual Violence*. New York, NY: John Wiley & Sons.

Maltz, W. (2001) *The Sexual Healing Journey: A Guide for Survivors of Sexual Abuse*. New York, NY: Quill.

Sanderson, C. (2006) *Counselling Adult Survivors of Child Sexual Abuse*. London: Jessica Kingsley Publishers.

Sanderson, C. (2009) *Introduction to Counselling Survivors of Interpersonal Trauma*. London: Jessica Kingsley Publishers.

Sanderson, C. (2015) *Counselling Skills for Working with Shame.* London: Jessica Kingsley Publishers.

Walker, P. (2013) *Complex PTSD: From Surviving to Thriving: A Guide and Map for Recovering from Childhood Trauma.* CreateSpace Independent Pub.

Resources for working with transgender survivors

Bean, L. (ed.) (2018) *Written on the Body: Letters from Trans and Non-Binary Survivors of Sexual Assault and Domestic Violence.* London: Jessica Kingsley Publishers.

Forge. Recoded webinars about a variety of topics related to supporting transgender survivors. Available at www.forge-forward. org/trainings-events/recorded-webinars.

Forge (2015) *Transgender Sexual Violence Survivors: A Self-Help Guide to Healing and Understanding.* Available at www.forge-forward.org/wp-content/docs/self-help-guide-to-healing-2015-FINAL.pdf.

Forge (2016) *A Guide for Facilitators of Transgender Community Groups: Supporting Sexual Violence Survivors.* Available at www. forge-forward.org/wp-content/docs/facilitators-guide-trans-support-groups.pdf.

Galop (2011) *Shining the Light: 10 Keys to Becoming a Trans Positive Organisation*. Available at www.galop.org.uk/wp-content/uploads/2011/05/final-shine-report-low-res.pdf.

Office for Victims of Crime Online Learning (2014) *Responding to Transgender Victims of Sexual Assault*. Available at www.ovc.gov/pubs/forge/index.html.

Patterson, J. (ed.) (2016) *Queering Sexual Violence*. New York, NY: Riverdale Avenue Books.

Rape Crisis Scotland (2011) *Stronger Together: Guidance for Women's Services on the Inclusion of Transgender Women*. Available at www.rapecrisisscotland.org.uk/resources/single-sex-service-trans-guidance.pdf.

Rape Crisis Scotland (2014) *Supporting LGBTI Survivors of Sexual Violence*. Available at www.rapecrisisscotland.org.uk/resources/RCS-001-LGBTI-A5booklet-02web.pdf.

Subject Index

Author Index